HIDDEN HISTORY *of* FORT COLLINS

HIDDEN HISTORY
of
FORT COLLINS

Barbara Fleming

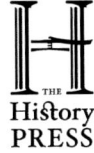

Published by The History Press
Charleston, SC
www.historypress.net

Copyright © 2017 by Barbara Fleming
All rights reserved

First published 2017

Manufactured in the United States

ISBN 9781625858948

Library of Congress Control Number: 2017945006

Notice: The information in this book is true and complete to the best of our knowledge. It is offered without guarantee on the part of the author or The History Press. The author and The History Press disclaim all liability in connection with the use of this book.

All rights reserved. No part of this book may be reproduced or transmitted in any form whatsoever without prior written permission from the publisher except in the case of brief quotations embodied in critical articles and reviews.

This book is dedicated to my readers, who over the years have let me know when I got it right and when I did not. They made this book possible.

Contents

Acknowledgements 9
Introduction 11
Who Came Before 13

1. The Wild West 15
2. Life on the Frontier 31
3. Memorable People 47
4. Law, Order and Public Safety 63
5. Frontier Education 80
6. Memorable Places, Local Landmarks 96
7. Some Twentieth-Century Tales 119

Bibliography 137
Index 139
About the Author 143

Acknowledgements

My thanks to those who graciously provided photographs—Marilyn Miller Van Ausdal, Stanley Sepulveda, Ed Lucero, Angeline Swets and Bill Swets.

As it has been with every local history book I have authored or coauthored, this book would not have happened without the help of the Local History Archive staff—Lesley Struc, archivist, and her assistants, Jennifer Hannifin and Jessica Gengler. My gratitude is boundless. Images provided by the Local History Archive are indicated by the initials LHA and the file number of the photograph.

My friend and coauthor Malcolm McNeil has again been immeasurably helpful in locating, providing and scanning photographs for this book. Thank you one more time, Mac. McNeil's images are indicated by his initials, MEM.

Thanks to the *Fort Collins Coloradoan* for letting me tell my stories in print.

Introduction

Fort Collins, Colorado, began as a military outpost along the path of westward migration. Its purpose was to protect settlers against Native Americans—sometimes with deadly outcomes. The fort existed from 1862 until it was decommissioned in 1867. Five years later, after the government had released the land, Franklin Avery platted a town along the Cache la Poudre River where soldiers had once been stationed.

During the early years the new town, which adopted the name of the military fort, experienced both heady growth and severe setbacks, finally emerging by the mid-1880s as a settled community with a stable government, law and order and a mostly upright citizenry. The town, today a mid-sized city, survived thanks to a legislative decision to establish an agricultural college on the site and the 1877 arrival of the railroad, right in the middle of the town, an amenity not appreciated by most residents now.

Colorful characters inhabit Fort Collins's early history, many of them well known: Jack Slade, a renegade said to have murdered more than thirty people (which he probably did not do, though he did kill a few) and hanged by a mob; Lady Catherine Moon, an Irish immigrant who began as a laundress and ended with a British title; Marie Lafitte, a feminist before her time who flaunted liquor laws and got away with it and then died a pauper; and Chief Friday Fitzpatrick, a Native American who was fluent in English and friends with many settlers, exiled to a reservation.

Of course, there are more stories than can be recounted here. Numerous historians have told the stories of memorable individuals and milestones of

Introduction

local history. The columns in this book, first published by the *Fort Collins Coloradoan* newspaper, and some shorter vignettes recount tales of people, of events, of culture and lifestyle, bringing together wide-ranging aspects of local history garnered from numerous sources—parts of our city's story that do not as often come to light.

History is people—their stories, framed in the context of their times. These stories can help in understanding and appreciating the times that came before our own, enriching and enlivening the culture.

Who Came Before

Long before the Wild West emerged in the nineteenth century, other people inhabited these lands. In 1927, A. Lynn Coffin and his father, Judge Roy Coffin, unearthed artifacts that established the presence of Paleo-Indian tribes about eleven thousand years ago, as evidenced by these Folsom points. In the 1930s, the Smithsonian Institute excavated the site. Today, it is part of the Fort Collins Soapstone Prairie Natural Area, where a buffalo herd thrives.

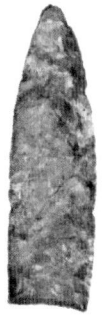

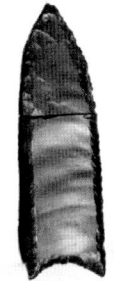

Folsom man weapon. *MEM.*

Chapter 1

The Wild West

Before the military outpost became a town, the Front Range of Colorado was part of the Wild West, with Native Americans fighting to save their hunting grounds, trappers roaming up and down the valley and canyon, cattle ranchers turning their herds loose in the hills and hunting rustlers when cattle disappeared. At the fort, the soldiers were occupied with their mission rather than with keeping general law and order, so settlers usually imposed their own version of justice.

As for Fort Collins, before the official settlement began in 1872, western culture and justice unquestionably prevailed. The town probably did not have an abundance of enticing women in fluffy dresses that revealed their legs, or pistol-packing cowpokes, or swinging saloon doors behind which a villain, only his hat and spurred boots showing, waited to create mayhem à la Hollywood, but there were plenty of weapons, plenty of accommodating women and enough saloons to satisfy everyone's thirst. Before emigrant women began to protest the drinking establishments, before churches were entrenched, this town was freewheeling and rough.

The streets were dirt, the sidewalks made of uneven boards. The buildings, many of them false-front structures, were made of wood. The prevailing odors were of horses, their droppings and whatever else arose from the dirt. Nearby, Chief Friday's Arapahos camped peaceably in winter, often coming into town in search of liquor or some other commodity. Trappers passing through traded their furs for goods and found in the town ample opportunity to let off steam. Settlers were self-sufficient for the most part, tending to their own business.

The tales that follow tell of the nineteenth-century Wild West, northern Colorado style, some of the tough, determined, hardy souls who lived through it and some who did not.

The Cherokee Trail

In 1849, a band of Cherokee set out for California hoping to find and mine gold. They had mined gold in Georgia, their native land, from which they had been forcibly relocated to Indian Lands, now Oklahoma. Finding no fortune or gold there, some among the tribe decided to head for California, where the fields supposedly gleamed with the precious metal.

Many of them were professionals—doctors, lawyers; most were well educated. Several kept diaries of the journey. Some Anglos joined the adventurers to create the large group that forged the Cherokee Trail. Historically, the Cherokee Trail starts at Bent's Fort in southeastern Colorado and ends at Fort Bridger in Wyoming, near the Utah border.

Starting on the well-worn Santa Fe Trail, the Cherokee party headed northwest toward Wyoming in order to circumvent the highest of the Rocky Mountains. Trails heading west generally bypassed Colorado because of that great obstacle—the Oregon Trail followed the North Platte through Nebraska to Wyoming. But the Cherokee party elected to skirt the mountains through eastern Colorado, following waterways as trails tended to do, when possible.

From Bent's Fort, established as a trading post in 1833, the trail headed northwest toward present-day Pueblo. Just south of present-day Franktown, the trail began following Cherry Creek and then the South Platte River. The trail followed the Poudre River north from Greeley, where it empties into the Platte. From Laporte, where the river could be crossed, the trail headed almost straight north. At approximately present-day Ted's Place, the intersection of U.S. Highways 287 and 14, it went toward Virginia Dale, thence westward toward Fort Bridger.

Near the Wyoming border, the Cherokee party parted ways, the main group heading almost due west and another group veering north and west through unknown territory. The break-off group heading north was composed of impatient young men—believing the train was moving too slowly, they traded their wagons for mules and ponies, slung packs on the mules and took off on their own, with limited provisions and no experienced guide. Later reports indicated that on the whole, they did not fare well.

The trail the Cherokees followed and forged was later widely used. In 1859, Horace Greeley wrote (as quoted in Lee Whitely's book *The Cherokee Trail*), "Cache la Poudre seems to be the center of the antelope country…no settlements save a small beginning just at the ford [Laporte]."

Even today, more than 150 years later, ruts from the Cherokee Trail still mark the land. Though the Oregon Trail is better known, the Cherokee Trail played a significant role in the opening of the West.

Mountain Men

Before civilization irrevocably encroached, the valley and canyon of the Poudre River had very few inhabitants—wildlife, Native American tribes and a particular type of loners who became known as mountain men. Mostly French-Canadian trappers, the latter had come to the area early in the nineteenth century.

They were muscular and sturdy, usually dressed in loose-hanging buckskin tunics belted at the waist and fringed on the sleeves and leggings, with long hair resting, unkempt, on broad shoulders and down the back, its color sun-bleached. From their belts hung pistols, and they were rarely without their long rifles. What skin was visible was leathery, wrinkled, browned by years of living outdoors. Some had prodigious mustaches, drooping down either side of the mouth, and tangled, untended beards. Eyes, ever watchful, peered out from beneath bushy eyebrows—their color slightly faded but the gaze keen. They wore worn leather boots and broad hats. Up close, they exuded a noticeable odor, garnered from the habit of bathing in creeks or streams only when the chance appeared (it being wise to stay close to clothes and a weapon), from frequent use of chewing tobacco and from infrequent but hearty imbibing of alcoholic beverages.

They spent their lives hunting game, sometimes hunting treasure, occasionally gambling with their earnings and carousing with others of their kind. Mostly they just wanted to be left alone to go their own ways, do as they wished and be obliged to no one.

Women would find them polite and respectful on the rare occasions when the two genders interacted, but they usually kept their distance, not knowing

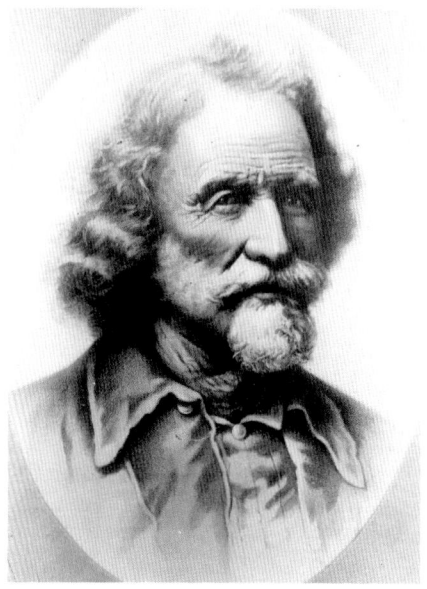 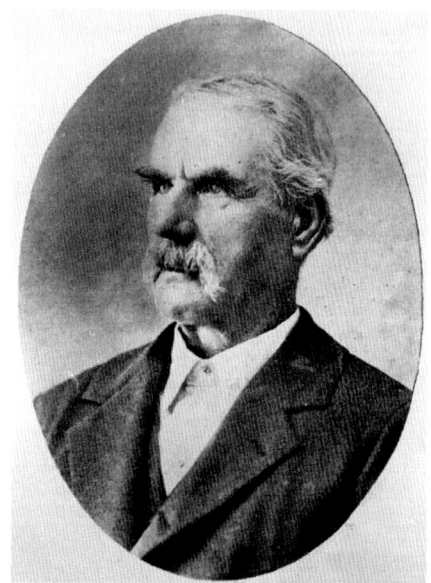

Left: Jim Baker, explorer, scout, interpreter, rancher. *LHA H11531*.

Right: John Provost, first settler in Laporte. *LHA H04380*.

how to behave or what to say and being alarmed by any possibility of closer contact—unless the woman had a specific purpose that they had sought out, a different circumstance altogether.

These men were not fictional creations or film caricatures. The mountain men who came west were very real, as colorful as anyone a person might hope to meet in a lifetime. A few names might be familiar—"Wild Bill" Hickok, Charley Utter (known as Colorado Charley) and Jim Nugent. These men lived by their own lights, proud of needing no one. They survived by killing and eating game and then selling their furs to buy ammunition and essentials like tobacco and coffee.

From time to time, mountain men would meet up at a trading post like Laporte to trade and sell their wares and chew the fat, but they never stayed in one place for long. Most were friendly with the Native Americans; some became bilingual or multilingual and could help novice travelers communicate. Some became scouts for the army or wagon trains. Some chose family life.

As did many others, John Provost married a Native American woman. He built what is considered the first cabin in Laporte, operated a ferry across the swift-running river and owned a grocery store and saloon. Unlike others, who continued to roam with their wives and families, he settled there.

Eventually, all the mountain men had to give up their way of life and learn to live with other people—not an easy transition at best.

The Wild West Was Here

Four men—George Pinkerton, Valentine Harstock, J.R. Todd and Thomas Gates—brought together a group of emigrants and adventurous young men to travel to the Territory of Oregon, setting out from Iowa in the spring of 1852. Years later, Todd told their story, recorded in Ansel Watrous's *History of Larimer County*.

Delayed by the army until the party was large enough—about three hundred people—the travelers headed westward until coming to the place where the Platte River divided into north and south forks. An established trail followed the North Fork through the Black Hills and then south again, but some among them wanted to seek a shorter route, so about seventy-five men decided to follow the South Fork. Soon they came upon the mouth of the Cache la Poudre River, which they followed northwest into Laporte (then called Colona).

Unsettled except by itinerant trappers and Native Americans, the valley they encountered seemed to be a "hunter's paradise." Buffalo herds roamed the grasslands; deer, elk and antelope abounded. The river teemed with fish; they caught trout all along the way. Coming upon Owl Canyon on the way north to Livermore, the men camped at the banks of the river.

They had seen Native Americans up on the bluffs above the valley, watching, so they increased the number of armed men guarding the cattle and horses. Though the night passed peaceably, in the morning the natives struck. One group went after the cattle, attacking the guards, while a second group went toward the wagons, "screeching like demons and beating dried deerskins and rattling deer hoofs and bones to stampede the stock."

It was an uneven contest. The attackers were armed only with bows and arrows and "a few old shotguns," while the defenders had loaded rifles and knew how to use them to the best effect. In about ten minutes the braves retreated, leaving behind nearly thirty of their dead and wounded. The traveling party lost two men, and two were wounded. They discovered some of their horses missing. Following the trail of the robbers, they came across some Native Americans, probably Utes, asleep by a campfire. The men recovered their horses, left the sleepers to their dreams and resumed their journey, soon to be joined by a band of Cherokee on their way to Oregon who said they had also been robbed by Utes. They continued their journey to the Virginia Dale stage station, an established stopping place on this westward route.

No one could say this journey was an easy one: they had to cut away dense underbrush and navigate slopes so steep they hitched ten oxen together to get just one wagon up mountainsides and tied wagon axles to trees to descend. But they made their destination "without further incident," records Watrous. He tells us no more.

Native American Attack

In the early 1850s, Robert Chambers was killed by Native Americans while camping with his son beside this natural lake high in Poudre Canyon. Upon returning from a supply run to town, his son, Robert Jr., found his father scalped and ridden with wounds, leaving evidence he had fought back as long as he could. The younger Chambers devoted his life to eradicating the entire native population. In the 1877 photograph on the following page, campers enjoy the canyon scenery on the shores of the lake named for the elder Chambers.

Is There Gold in Them Thar Hills?

Stagecoach driver George Pritchett and guard Albert "Frenchy" LeBlanc knew they were running a risk when they set out, carrying gold, without a military escort on June 10, 1872. But they weren't really concerned—both hardened mountain men, they were crack shots quite able to shoot to kill. What was there to worry about?

Plenty, as it turned out.

Escorted by cavalry, the coach had arrived safely at the Namaqua stage station near Loveland, their precious cargo intact. But in the morning when they prepared to set out again, Colonel Oscar Critchell informed them that the army escort designated to complete the journey was away,

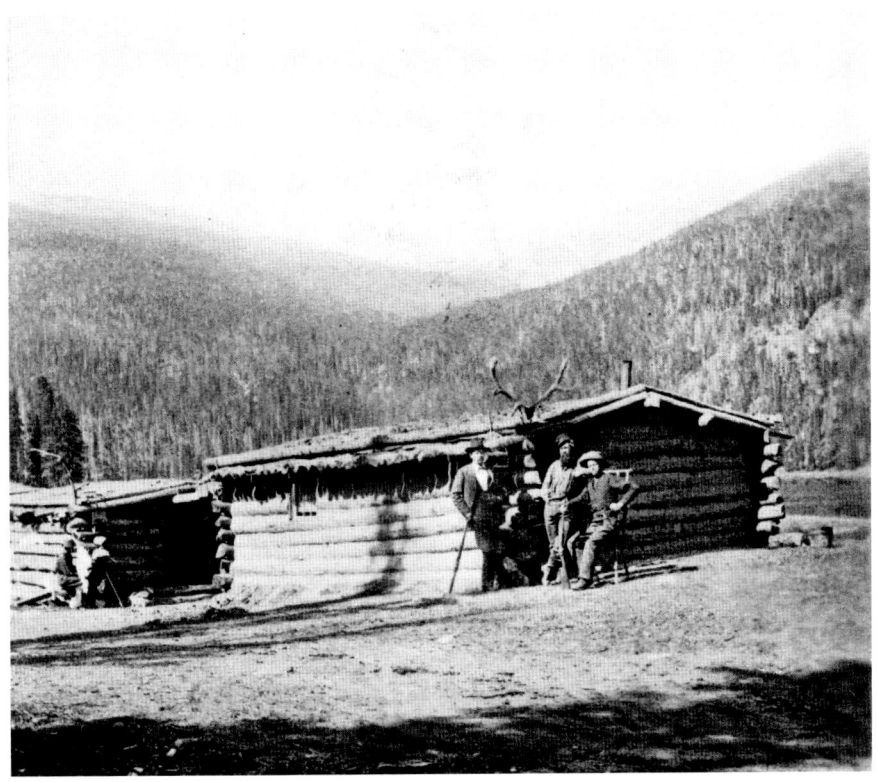

Camp on Chambers Lake. *MEM.*

pursuing Utes. It could be a few days before they returned; delivery of the army payroll would have to wait.

Nope, said Pritchett. They could make it without the soldiers. Reluctantly, Critchell agreed. Pritchett and LeBlanc set out toward Fort Laramie. They had not gone far, though, when the Borrell Gang, father and sons, spotted the coach. No heads of passengers visible, no luggage on top—clearly, the coach was carrying something else, something valuable. Lurking behind boulders, the robbers fatally shot the driver and his guard, calmed the panicked mules, grabbed the lockbox containing the gold coins and absconded into the hills to escape the soldiers they expected any minute.

Indeed, the cavalry was in hot pursuit. Regretting his decision, Critchell had dispatched troops to find the coach and escort it even though his men were not supposed to go that far north. The troops arrived just as the brothers were sprinting away. Ordered to stop, the gang kept running, getting far enough away to hide their booty—only afterward to encounter the Fourth Frontier cavalry troops returning from their pursuit of Utes. Confronted with weapons, the soldiers fired, killing all four gang members. One brother, Cobe, lived long enough to refuse, profanely, to tell the soldiers where the loot was hidden.

For weeks soldiers searched the hills along what is now U.S. 287, to no avail. Then civilians came by the hundreds, again with no success—until August 1883, when rancher Stacy Wehrer came jauntily down a hill on horseback one day and happened upon a group of rough-looking men who demanded to know why he was smiling. "Nice day," he replied, but not quite casually enough. The gangsters became convinced he was up to something when Wehrer suddenly kicked his mount and tried in vain to rush past the men. After they shot him, they found eleven double eagles (twenty-dollar gold coins) in his pocket. He'd discovered the treasure! But even as he lay dying, he would not reveal its location.

So where's the gold? It must be somewhere. The money was in the stagecoach; then it was gone. The Borrell Gang stole the money; then they hid it. Wehrer later found some of it; then he died, his secret untold. What remains, now worth millions, has yet to be found after more than one hundred years. Will it ever be?

Winter March

The weather was bright and clear on the January day in 1865 when Captain James Hanna led about seventy soldiers of the Eleventh Ohio Cavalry from Fort Laramie to Fort Collins to reinforce Major William Evans's troops there. Clad only in buckskin, buffalo and beaver skins, the men rode along cheerfully, confident of arriving in good time.

But as they lay sleeping on the first night, it began to snow. When they woke in the morning, everything around them was dazzling white, and the temperature had dropped considerably. They could not turn back; they had to keep going toward their destination. And they did—headlong into a full-blown winter blizzard. The snow whirled around them, blinding them; the horses bent their heads against the sharp, fiercely cold snowflakes. The wind cut through them like a knife. It kept getting colder. They stayed close together, no one daring to fall behind. They well knew that wolves awaited such tempting prey.

The empty, treeless plain offered no shelter. According to one soldier who recounted the event years later, as recorded in Ansel Watrous's *History of Larimer County*, no houses could be found between the two forts, nor was there a trail to follow. They were alone in a vast, empty, frigid wilderness.

At last they came to a likely spot and made camp, such as it was. Exhausted, disheartened and freezing, the horses lay down in the snow, seeming to understand their fate. Only their heads jutted up above the blankets of snow. As for the men, they spooned as close together as they could get, getting as warm as possible under blankets and snow. Regularly, the sergeant-at-arms would call out, "Spoon!" and as one they would roll to the other side without letting in the cold. It was, said the old soldier, "a night of horrors"—with more to come.

In the morning, they had to force themselves to keep going. Men were getting frostbite; horses were flagging and dropping down to feed the wolves. Some men appeared close to death, but their companions would not let them die, forcing them to walk or run until the deadly lethargy left them. Another day, another "hideous" night, the mercury about thirty below. Finally, the captain ordered the supply wagons dismantled for firewood. The men soon had a roaring fire to warm themselves and make some coffee. Alas, the fire did not last long; the wind blew it all away, ashes, embers and all.

On the fourth day, having abandoned all their supplies and most of the horses, the soldiers experienced what to them was a miracle: the sun came out. It did not warm the air much, but the storm was over. They knew, then, that they would make it.

It was a ragged, frostbitten, bone-tired group of soldiers, men of iron will and boundless courage, who staggered at last into their new home to recover from their ordeal and prepare to go out and do their duty all over again.

What Became of Happy Jack?

He was known only as Happy Jack, a drifter who stole horses, assaulted women and lived by his wits. In 1873, he made his way to the Fort Collins area.

Ansel Watrous relates Happy Jack's tale. At first, he sought work in a mill, but he was soon found to be "not of much account" as a millworker, so he entered into a life of crime. In those days, the worst possible crime was stealing horses, and Jack was accused of doing just that. In time, Sheriff Joe

Mason, arrest warrant in hand, caught up with him and brought him back to Fort Collins for trial.

However, Happy Jack was released due to insufficient evidence. He promptly left town, heading for the hills. Arriving at the Gilpin-Brown ranch, he found a woman alone and asked her to cook a meal for him. She did, but she paid for her kindness with a cruel assault that left her semi-conscious. She later told her husband that during the meal the assailant had inquired the way to Rabbit Creek, so the sheriff headed that direction, but in fact Jack had ridden due west. He stopped at another ranch for milk; the man who provided it soon learned that he had helped a fugitive and informed Mason. Not long after that, the sheriff and his deputy came upon Jack, sound asleep, and apprehended him.

The miscreant in tow, the two men started back to town. On the way, they stopped at the Day cabin on the Gilpin-Brown ranch and asked Mrs. Day to identify Jack as her assailant, which she did. Sheriff Mason then roped Jack to a post, handed Mrs. Day his rifle and invited her to shoot him. Though she must have been tempted, she could not bring herself to pull the trigger, so the sheriff continued on into town.

When the prisoner refused to give up any of his horse-thieving cohorts, he was brought to the jail in the courthouse, given a meal, manacled and then left to the care of a prison guard. Before long, Happy Jack started complaining that one of the manacles was too tight, so the guard loosened them, fastening them to Jack's boots. Soon the prisoner had worked his feet out of the boots. Somehow he wriggled out of the window in the cell and took off into the night.

Although a posse was quickly mounted, Jack had planned his escape well. It was dark, and the small settlement offered many hiding places. He got away and "was never seen in this vicinity again"—leaving behind, notes Watrous, true Wild West stories to be recounted years later by old-timers and a mystery that was never solved: what became of Happy Jack?

Letters from the Post

"Affectionate wife," begins a letter dated December 15, 1865, written by Hiram Barney while he was stationed at Fort Collins in Colorado Territory.

Barney, mustered a corporal out of the army, wrote faithfully to his wife, Mary, in Rochester, New York. He would have liked, he told her, to see a buffalo, but they were all gone from the prairie, having "fled from the unerring rifle of the white men to more congenial quarters." He wrote to his daughter, Ella, that he was making finger rings for her out of beef bones and buffalo horns.

Though he had not seen any buffalo in spite of his "strong desire" to do so, Barney commented that he had seen antelope, rabbits, deer, mountain sheep, prairie dogs, wolves and prairie chickens and had eaten the meat of some of them.

In letters written during the particularly cold and bitter winter of 1865–66, he laments the fact that his bunkmate had already left, leaving him to sleep alone. On such cold nights, soldiers would spoon together during the night to use one another's bodies for warmth. "Oh, how I do pitty [sic] the poor soldier sentinel as he walkes [sic] his beat these cold nights. What do you think wife, a guard in front of headquarters froze his hand and cheeks yesterday."

To entertain themselves on long winter evenings, the soldiers sang, talked and read, and after payday, some played a card game of "bluff" (probably poker) in which Hiram did not partake, for he had stashed his earnings inside an inner shirt pocket and refused to lend money to any of his companions, telling them it was in a bank. He had, he related, seen some bad loans, and experience had taught him to avoid such borrowers "as you would a venomous reptile."

And concerning reptiles, Barney told of encountering large rattlesnakes in the area. One had eight rattles.

"Everything is high here," he remarked, "so it will not do to buy much only what is actually needed." He dreamed of opening his own grocery store when he got home and assured his "dear wife" that "it is not long ere I shall be with you."

At last, on June 19, 1866, Barney wrote to his wife that he was on his way home. The soldiers were given $100 for transportation—"more than enough." Frugal as ever, he was traveling across the plains with two companions, all armed. "I am a different man physically since I have been in the army and there are very few men I am afraid to confront," he assured her, no doubt so she would not worry while he was on the homeward journey.

A letter written on July 3 on the way to Julesburg ends longingly with "till we meet, accept of a husband's love, Hiram."

One Who Stayed

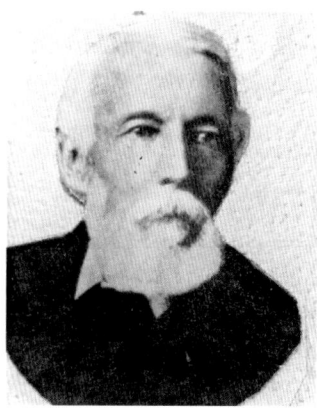

George Buss. *LHA H06662B.*

George Buss fought for the Union at Bull Run, Chancellorsville and Antietam and came to Camp Collins in 1865. After mustering out, he decided to stay and bought land near Timnath, then sent for his family in New York.

Buss was not alone in his decision to return to the valley; a number of other soldiers based at the fort also brought their families here after arriving at home.

Roundup

Every fall, itinerant cowboys gathered together, hired by ranchers to do the annual roundup, catching cattle grazing freely, herding them together and driving them to market. It was a unique time that the cowboys, usually independent loners, must have looked forward to.

They would have heard the cattle, munching on grass and communicating softly with one another, their *moos* intelligible only to others of their species. In the vast silence of the hillside, these sounds would have carried long distances. The *moos* mingled with the sounds of the horses, tails swishing to drive away the flies, occasional snorts and *whuffs* wafting through the still air. In the distance, a coyote's howl might have pierced the silence, saying that it smelled the cattle and was weighing the chance to bring one down.

Before dark, the hardworking crew would have enjoyed a hearty meal of beans, corn bread and crisp fried potatoes. The food would have been especially relished because they had worked all day, not stopping for a noon meal. Late-summer days are long and hot, and it would have been many hours since their breakfast of boiled coffee, thick and bitter, and fluffy biscuits.

After the meal, some would lie on the grass, propped by an elbow, periodically spitting out tobacco. Some sat on their haunches and twined rope, while others smoked in silence. Now and then a cowboy might break into song, favorites being mournful tunes about love and loss. One man might have a guitar.

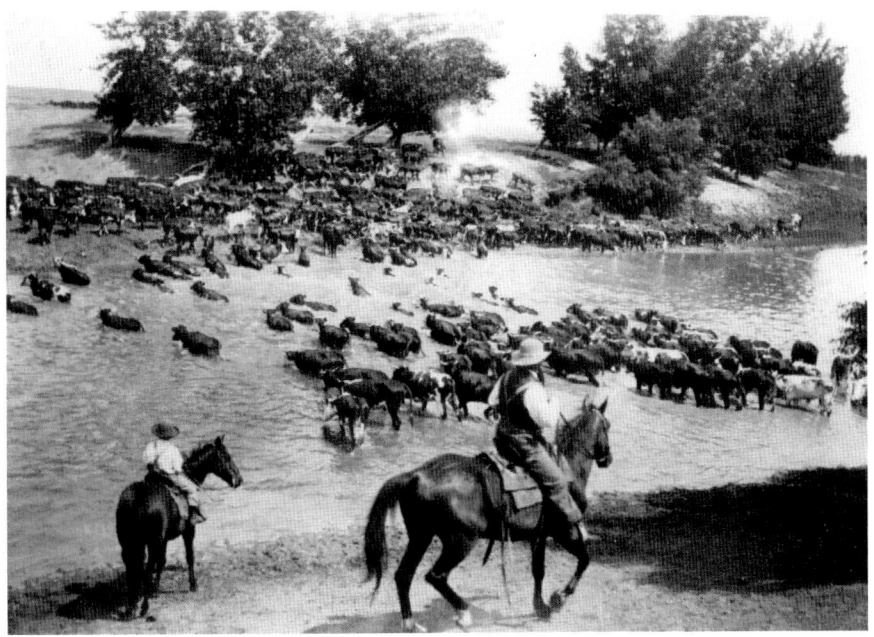

Roundup. *LHA H03385.*

Sometimes they could persuade the resident poet (there was nearly always such a man among them) to recite poetry cowboys favored, about the creatures with them on the roundup, about the trail, about loneliness, about lost loves and not infrequently about death.

When night fell, one cowboy, armed, would be assigned to guard the herd while the rest slept on the ground, saddles or saddle blankets under their heads. In a few hours, he would wake a comrade and take his turn sleeping under the stars while his buddy sat with a rifle across his legs, watchful.

The black sky would have been thick with stars, many more stars than are visible in most places now, with no light to dim their brilliance. The fire would have been damped down, even the tiniest flame dead, for if a stray wind-blown spark were to start a wildfire there would be chaos, panic, disaster.

At dawn, the day's work would begin again.

The era of roundups like this—wrangling cattle, roping and branding them, herding them to market—was brief but intense, perhaps later remembered by the tough men who experienced it, surely romanticized by those who looked back on it and barely imaginable by us today.

Advice for Stagecoach Travelers

It is to be hoped that first-time passengers on a Concord stagecoach prepared well and heeded advice from experienced travelers before setting out for what was, at best, an ordeal.

The coach seated nine people on three seats, but early arrivals got the best seats. Least desirable was the middle seat, which had only a strap at the back. Three people squeezed into a space about four feet wide didn't leave much room for each person—but on the other hand, a tight fit would help hold everyone steadier. Going along trails that were not really roads, just rutted tracks packed down to hard dirt by wagon wheels and horses' hooves, meant a bumpy ride, so hanging on was essential. Bundles of mail on the floor left little leg room. (Luggage was tied on top.)

The coach traveled about ten miles and then stopped at a way station to change horses. Going that fast, they tired quickly. At the station, passengers could freshen up a bit (outdoor pump with ice-cold water, fireplace indoors), get some sustenance (hardly gourmet fare, probably bad coffee) and stretch their legs, which they would be grateful to do. Any food passengers brought along had to be shared. In such close quarters, there was no other choice. And they might well have hoped no one lit a cigar.

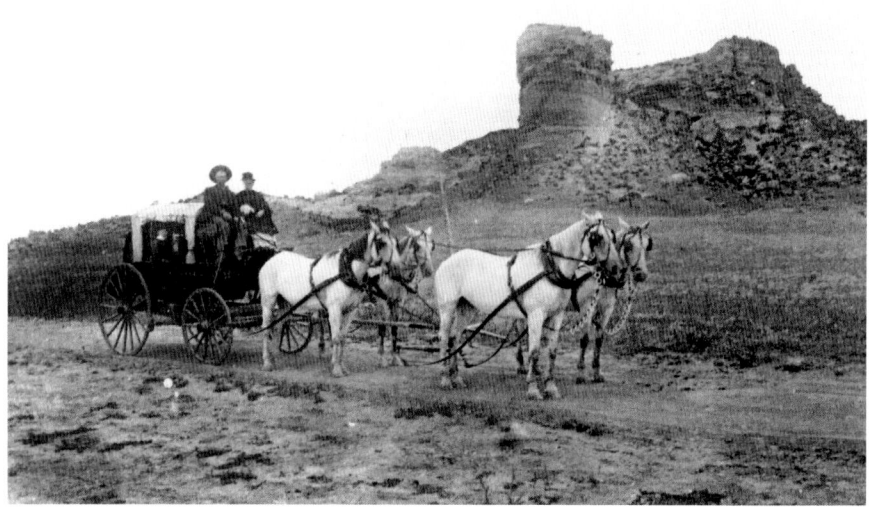

Stagecoach—not the most comfortable way to travel. *LHA H08220.*

As for clothing, the weather could change very suddenly, and the coach provided little protection. The horses raised considerable dust, so wise passengers would wear bandanas to protect their mouths and noses.

Passengers might have been apprehensive about mishaps, but they were rare. The driver and conductor were well armed, able to use their firearms in the event of an attack or a robbery, both of which were possible but not probable. Such things happened much less often than Hollywood would have people believe. Ben Holladay's Overland Stage Company claimed to be 100 percent reliable, and mostly it was. Still, passengers who arrived safe and sound must have been relieved, grateful to be once again on solid ground.

The Story of Jimmy Kelly

When picnickers and campers select a campground along the Poudre River in the canyon, they might wonder for a moment why it has a particular name. Take Kelly Flats, for example.

In his book *Cache la Poudre, The River*, early settler Norman Fry tells the story of Jimmy Kelly, a one-time worker in logging camps who, unlike most others, chose to stick around when the railroad-tie industry began dying out in the late 1880s. He and Jack Dunn, another tie hack, decided to join forces and build bachelor cabins along a mountain creek.

Dunn worked for Charles Andrews at Kinikinik, farther northwest, building fences and constructing ditches, but that work ran out after a while, so he returned to his cabin. "Somehow," says Fry, "it mysteriously burned down," leaving Dunn to move in with Kelly. Kelly had a three-room cabin, sizeable for its time, and a herd of fifteen burros. Fry describes him as a small, "picturesque" man who dressed himself in clothes made from skins of animals that he had hunted.

Canyon residents thought Dunn would outwit Kelly and get the cabin, but one night they fought, and Kelly "got the drop" on Dunn, forcing him onto a chair and keeping him there at gunpoint all night. In the morning, Dunn took all his worldly goods and departed for parts unknown.

Kelly's canny nature, which Fry calls "unscrupulous," came to light while he was providing a nearby ditch camp with what he called elk meat. But when he began his fall round-up, John Zimmerman discovered a number of his cattle missing. Hmmm. (In retrospect, it is surprising that workers at the ditch camp did not notice that they were eating beef rather than elk; the flavors are distinctly different.)

In the spring of 1894, Kelly made a tactical error. He killed a dog belonging to the La Fever ranch, and he threatened Mrs. La Fever. The next time he rode by, Abe La Fever was waiting for him. In effect, he told Kelly to leave the area or suffer the consequences—so Kelly moved on, despite the fact that La Fever was unarmed. One wonders about the nature of the rancher's threat; rustling, after all, was a hanging offense at that time. It seems likely that Kelly was well aware of the consequence he might face.

Without doubt, Jimmy Kelly was one of the more colorful characters to inhabit the Poudre Canyon in the nineteenth century. Today, its lively past obscured by time, the area—not all flat by any means—is a popular campground in Roosevelt National Forest that features a hiking trail nicknamed "heart attack hill" because of its abrupt, steep ascent.

Chapter 2

LIFE ON THE FRONTIER

Deciding to claim land, plat a town and advertise for settlers is one thing; achieving success at that venture is quite another. In the early days of Fort Collins, the town's future was anything but assured.

Before the military land was released by the government in 1872, there had been some settlement around the fort; a small commercial area had developed along the riverfront. Cabins were scattered here and there. Once the land was available, a group of businessmen put together a plan for the new town, naming it the Agricultural Colony. Franklin Avery laid out the streets. But the little town had a very long way to go. In the first year of its existence, the platted area did fill to a degree, but many potential residents were driven off by the continuing drought and the consequent invasion of grasshoppers, an invasion so devastating that some fields were stripped completely dry.

Fort Collins (which it soon became, the name change historically murky) was intended to be a center for agricultural commerce, supporting the farmers who would homestead and farm around it. A drought severe enough to discourage farmers was not an auspicious start. Then, to top it off, the town's first bank failed. Yet there remained hardy folks who refused to give up. After all, the town had been chosen by the territorial legislature as the site for a land grant college, which would assure a future, and people like Elizabeth Stone and James Arthur believed in that future enough to invest in it.

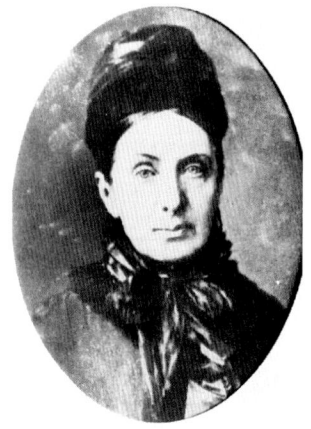

British explorer Isabella Bird. *LHA H12365.*

Still, living in Fort Collins in the early days was a struggle that required both faith and investment. Explorer Isabella Bird, passing through in 1872, found the place "revolting," with "coarse speech, coarse food, coarse everything." It is within that environment that this chapter dwells, sharing stories of early pioneer troubles and triumphs.

Invasion

They came (by the millions), they saw (anything remotely edible), they ate (voraciously, everything in sight).

In 1873, hordes of grasshoppers darkened the skies, the noise of their whirring wings blotting out all other sounds. Landing in fields and yards, they consumed vegetation down to bare soil—stems, leaves, fruit, every morsel. The sounds of their chomping were deafening.

Homemakers were afraid to hang up their clothes outdoors because the hoppers ate them. Sometimes they even ate the rope the clothes hung on. Children could not play outdoors; livestock was constantly plagued by the pesky insects.

Ill prepared to combat the invasion, which had been exacerbated by a prolonged drought, the farmers could do little but watch and wait as their crops disappeared before their very eyes. What were people and their animals to eat? How would they get through the winter? Discouraged, many settlers gave up and moved on to what they hoped were greener pastures.

These swarms of pests came hard on the heels of another catastrophe—a recent arrival named Harry Tutton had started a bank downtown. The institution thrived for a time, until a nationwide financial panic swept through Colorado, closing many banks and businesses. Tutton went to Denver one day, supposedly to retrieve some surplus funds he had deposited in another bank there, and he never came back. No one seemed to know what had become of him, but one thing was certain: the bank was defunct; much of the settlers' money was gone. And to add to their woes, grasshoppers were devouring the countryside.

What could be done? There were no airplanes with insecticide to call on for relief, and the study of best agricultural practices was in its infancy then.

According to *History of Larimer County*, the early 1870s were "a gloomy period" in our history. What Watrous called "the grasshopper years" nearly wiped out our fledgling little settlement.

But not quite. By 1874, farmers were more prepared for the great grasshopper invasion, more able to save at least some of their crops with irrigation. Those who hung on did achieve small harvests despite the insects.

It is to the ones who remained, "with stouter hearts, more courage and more means," as Watrous describes them, and the ones who came and decided to stay, that we owe the survival of Fort Collins. For reasons known only to the grasshoppers (and no doubt to individuals conversant in these matters), they did not come again in such numbers between 1876, when a growth period of peace and prosperity began, and 1911, when Watrous published his history.

Other factors contributed to the resurgence of prosperity in Fort Collins—mainly, the establishment of an agricultural college and the arrival of the railroad—but these events do not detract from the amazing fortitude of those few settlers who believed in a brighter future and chose to stay around to help make it happen.

The Most Dreaded Event

More than winter blizzards or summer storms, more than drought or insect invasions, more than restless natives or outlaws, frontier settlers feared fire. It's easy to see why. Most buildings were made of wood, and much of the frontier was (and is) not humid, so wood dried out quickly. Worse, the weapons to fight fire were limited. Once started—by a spark from a fireplace or stove or by an overturned kerosene lamp, perhaps by a smoldering cigar left unattended—fire was ruthless and voracious. The goal was not so much to put out a fire as to keep it from spreading.

When a fire began, the alarm went throughout the town—a bell or someone running through the streets—and people poured out of their houses or businesses, buckets at the ready. Lines formed. Water was drawn from the nearest source (here, the river or a ditch) and the full bucket exchanged for an empty one, up the line, until it reached the fire, where it was tossed at the flames, the ant attacking the rubber tree plant. On and on the bucket brigade struggled (no hoses or water hydrants). Weary dippers at the water end gave way to fresher ones. Those closest to the fire were in danger of singed hair or skin or of falling, burning debris. The heat was searing (no helmets or protective gear). Attention was paid to nearby buildings to contain the fire. It seemed to be hours before the fire was subdued at last.

This scenario occurred over and over again, from coast to coast but especially on the western frontier, until more modern firefighting methods were developed.

On Tuesday, February 3, 1880, disaster struck here when the Welch Block (building) at the corner of College and Mountain Avenues caught fire. The store on the first floor and rooms on the second were all consumed by the hungry flames. Jacob Welch (the owner), his wife and their grandchild and Dr. Timothy Smith, his wife and two children all escaped, but when the fire was out, the bodies of A.F. Hopkins and Tillie Irving, both clerks at the store, were discovered. Watrous calls this "the darkest hour the town had seen in its history." The effect on the community was profound.

Clearly, better fire protection was essential. In May of that year, a hook and ladder company was formed; town officials supplied equipment. Officers were appointed, bylaws adopted and preparations for more effective firefighting begun. Fort Collins progressed to horse-drawn water wagons, hoses and pumps and well-trained firefighters. (Horses once were stabled in the very back of what is now Old Firehouse Bookstore on Walnut Street.)

No doubt confident that calamity would not strike again, Welch rebuilt the same year, constructing the first three-story building in Fort Collins. Fire did happen again there a few years later, but the town's "very efficient fire department" was ready and able to deal with it.

Justice on the Frontier

On July 4, 1879, in Fort Collins as elsewhere, people celebrated with speeches, music and a parade, ending with a fireworks display at dark, the first such display held here, according to Ansel Watrous. Along toward dusk, three men who had been working on the Larimer and Weld Canal came into town for a little revelry.

At the time Fort Collins was not a dry town, and the young men, says Watrous, "proceeded to fill themselves up with booze." They soon became loud and obnoxious "with their loud talk and swaggering ways." At length, one of them pulled a paper balloon around his body as if it were a petticoat, offending some sensibilities beyond endurance, so the sheriff and the town marshal took them into custody.

Where to put them? There was not yet a city jail, and the magistrate was out of town. The next-best choice, the officers decided, was to take them to Frank Stover's store, Stover being a town trustee. The officers reasoned that if he did not actually have legal authority to try them for disturbing the peace, he ought to have had it; therefore, necessity prevailed. Agreeing with their somewhat shaky premise, Stover accepted the challenge, but since there was not much room in his store, which was then housed in part of a bank building, he moved the proceedings out into the street, using an upended barrel in lieu of a desk. A crowd quickly gathered to witness the "trial."

The young men, described by Watrous as tenderfeet unfamiliar with "wild, Western ways for dealing with justice," quickly sobered up. They feared the outcome—would they be strung from the nearest tree? They could, comments Watrous, almost picture their lifeless bodies swinging in the wind. Where was the compassion? Was anyone sorry for their plight? Would no one save them? Seeing no sympathy among the crowd and only a stern expression on the face of the presiding judge, they despaired for their lives. Trembling with terror, they threw themselves on the mercy of the court, promising to leave town promptly, never to cause any more trouble, if only they would be spared.

At length, having had his fun, Stover fined them $5.00 and costs. Alas, they could only come up with $1.35 among the three of them. The court accepted the payment and let the miscreants depart, which they wasted no time in doing. For all we know, they never came back to the unruly frontier town.

The festivities resumed. When the evening ended and the crowd dispersed, everyone who'd been there had a great story to tell on the morrow.

An Old West Valentine's Story

"Wanted: At Fort Collins, Colorado, about 50 unmarried ladies between the ages of 18 and 40, sound of limbs, wind and bustle, by uxorious bachelors and widowers of this city. Husbands and homes guaranteed. No crusaders need apply." This advertisement appeared in the *Dial* newspaper in Boscobel, Wisconsin, on August 18, 1874, and was reprinted in the local newspaper in 1959 with the headline "You've Missed Your Chance by 85 Years."

Who placed this advertisement? No one knows. Clearly, they were motivated by a severe shortage of women in Fort Collins. What sorts of "crusaders" did these lonely men not want? Given the amount of free-flowing liquor in our town then, probably temperance supporters.

In 1874, our town was on the cusp of becoming civilized—but not quite there yet. Saloons abounded, establishments featuring women of the pecuniary persuasion flourished and churches were few. Though there were no shootouts à la the film *High Noon* in Fort Collins, odds are that at least some men walking the streets here were armed.

On the other hand, there was a small public school, and plans were underway for the agricultural college. The town had a lawyer, a bank and a sheriff to maintain law and order.

What, one wonders, would lure women seeing this advertisement to pack up their belongings and head westward into an unknown abyss? Little accurate information had drifted east about the lands Lewis and Clark had explored decades earlier. What the advertisement's readers knew—or thought they knew—probably came from romanticized tales of adventures, overblown newspaper reports and idealized landscape paintings they might have seen. They did not, after all, have the Internet available to look up their destination—or match.com to view the men. Moreover, it would be a long, fatiguing journey. Even the trip from Denver to Fort Collins would take two days along rutted, dusty roads.

Did any women respond to this enticing prospect of "home and husband"? Here and there a widow, perhaps, or a young woman yearning for adventure, or a spinster unable to find an eligible man in Boscobel and eager to enter the married state. Whoever they were, if the advertisement actually brought some women here, they would have become joined to men sight unseen until the moment of their arrival in Fort Collins. Perhaps letters were exchanged first. What if a widow brought children with her? No mention is made of correspondence or children. Would the petitioners pay their passage west? Again, the advertisement makes no such promise. And "sound of limbs, wind and bustle" hints of hard work ahead. What about sound of mind?

The curious are left with only questions, interest piqued by this optimistic little piece in a small-town (population about 1,500) newspaper long, long ago.

Our Town's First Photographer

Mrs. E.A. Masters (given name unknown, due to the journalistic custom of the times) arrived in Fort Collins sometime in 1874, as nearly as is known. In his book *Early Photographers of Fort Collins*, Malcolm McNeill tells her story.

Not only was she a photographer, Mrs. Masters was an experienced telegrapher, and Fort Collins had high hopes of gaining a telegraph line in aid of communication with the eastern half of the nation. McNeill speculates that she might have hoped that having the job of telegrapher in combination with her nascent photography business would keep her solvent, for as a single source of income her photography was not sufficient in such a small town.

She intended to open her new gallery in May 1874, but unfortunately, she suffered a severe setback. On May 20, the *Rocky Mountain News* reported a carriage accident as she and Jacob Welch were on their way to Greeley. The horse apparently being of volatile temperament, she was thrown from the carriage and sustained some minor wounds. But then, inexplicably, the two passengers decided to try again—same carriage, same horse—a few days later, and this time she was not so lucky. After several days, she appeared in town on crutches, recovering from a broken leg.

Undaunted, she carried on with her plans. The telegraph line was routed from Cheyenne to Denver via Fort Collins, south from here through other towns and then to points east. On September 23, 1874, the new telegraph line was completed. "We can communicate with the world by lightning," stated the *Fort Collins Standard* newspaper. Headquarters for the operation was Mrs. Masters's new gallery, the first photography studio in town.

This energetic entrepreneur offered lessons in telegraphic technique and filled her gallery with a wide variety of her own photographs. Business was brisk, the newspaper reported, but times were tight, so she was willing to barter in lieu of cash, a common practice at that time.

By 1877, Fort Collins had trains, requiring telegraph lines to send messages about track switches, arrival times and other vital information. So when the Colorado Central Railroad arrived, the local telegraph operation relocated to the station next to the tracks. Mrs. Masters lost an important source of income.

With such a leap of progress, the newspaper seems to have lost interest in her, for McNeill found no further information, only that in July 1878, her studio had new occupants, James Shipler and Milton Williamson. Unable to make a living here any longer, she must have moved on to greener fields, so to speak, but one hopes she continued to take pictures. Considering the high praise she had gotten while in business here, wherever she went they no doubt would have been fine indeed.

Then Came the Bicycle

Women loved the bicycle, which necessitated wearing split skirts or pantaloons and offered them freedom they had never had before. They quickly formed riding clubs. Along with this new mode of transportation came bicycle repair shops like this one, photographed in 1908 somewhere downtown. No doubt it was one of several scattered around the town. The first bicycle, called a penny-farthing, had a very high back wheel and small front wheel, making it a challenge to ride, but people did.

"Where Man Had Never Gone Before"

Towering high above the valley below, Long's Peak had become a mountain to conquer even as early as 1871. For that is when the Reverend Elkanah Lamb set out with a party of eight to reach the top. It was August, a good time for climbing, but of his party, Lamb was the only one to make it all the way.

For a little while, he savored the conquest and the view. Then he made what could have been a fatal decision. He would go down the east face, "where man had never gone before," instead of descending the way he had come. Years later he wrote, "I began to realize the rashness of the undertaking." He had already made his way through "perpendicular places, ice patches and frowning walls," but here he was confronted with sloping ice. He pondered going back up to descend the way he had come, but the ice was too slippery. Climbing up was impossible. His only choice was to keep going down.

He was alone, without the climbing gear considered essential today. The air was thin and cold. He put his fingers into a tiny hole, pressing his feet against the icy wall to get a foothold. But then, "quicker than I can tell it, my hands failed to hold, my feet slipped, and down I went."

After falling several feet, he managed to get one arm around a projecting rock, bringing him to a sudden stop. His life, his wife, his home filled his

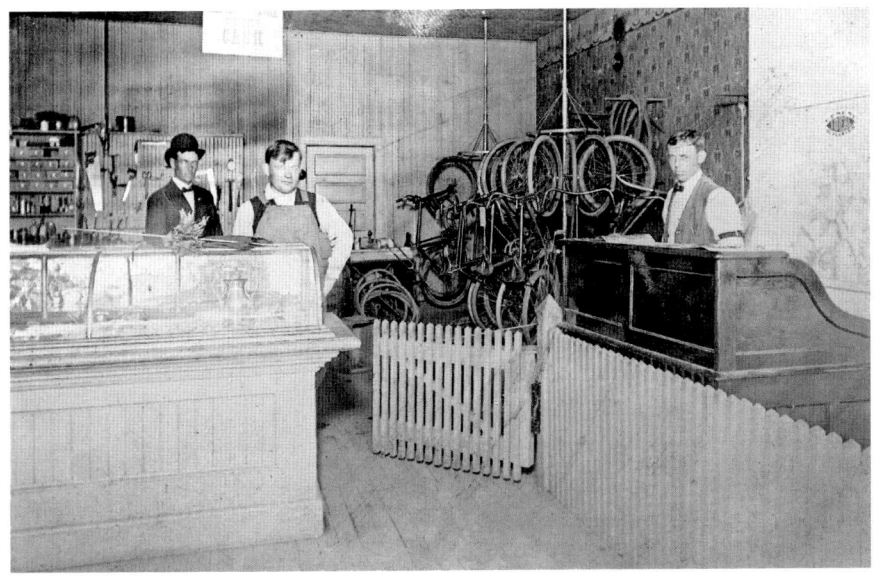

A bicycle repair shop somewhere downtown. *MEM.*

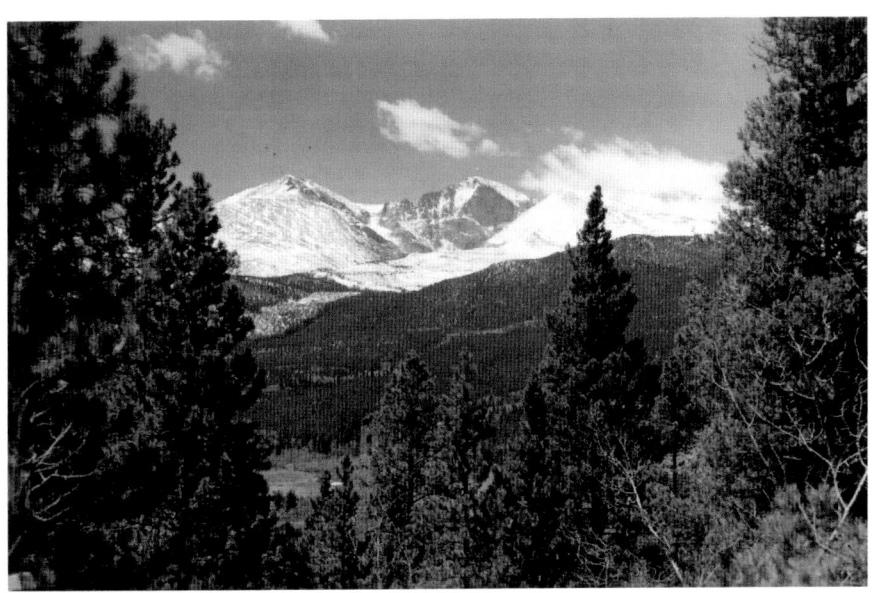

Long's Peak, named for Major Stephen Long. *LHA Ha4079.*

mind as he contemplated a grisly end. But he didn't give up. Somehow, he got a knife out of his pocket, opened it with his teeth and dug a toehold. His knife broke in half.

A moment later, he lunged forward and slid down a considerable distance before attaining an area where rocks projected enough that he could grip with his hands and feet from one to another. At last he reached the foot of the mountain, still sound of limb and full of thankfulness.

A preacher with the United Brethren, Lamb had been bringing his message to settlers in the Estes Park area for a time before his famous descent. But the financial rewards were slim, so eventually he claimed a homestead and built a lodge for visitors, many of whom he guided up Long's Peak and safely back down again. He wrote, "If they would not pay for spiritual guidance, I compelled them to pay for material elevation."

Lamb's descent is now known as Lamb's Slide, an eight-hundred-foot, seventy-degree, ice-covered slope. His extraordinary feat held until 1903, when his nephew, Enos Mills, often called the father of Rocky Mountain National Park, replicated it. Since then, some climbers have died trying; others have failed or been injured. Whoever might have succeeded him, however, Lamb did it first.

Courtship and Justice, Frontier Style

In 1878, when the Arapaho tribe that had been living near Fort Collins was confined to the Pine Ridge Reservation in South Dakota, young William "Billy" Provost and his brother, John Provost, went with their mother to her new home. Her husband, John Provost, an early settler in Laporte, had elected to remain in Laporte in order to retain his property here, as the government had decreed.

The younger John, who spoke English, took a job as interpreter at the reservation. There resided in the village a beautiful young maiden, Soeteiva (Little Bird), and both Provost youths fell in love with her, relates Ansel Watrous in his Larimer County history. Billy decided to court her.

The tribal custom was that the prospective groom would bring a horse to the bride's father as a "bride price" to win her hand. Alas, Billy did not have a horse. But Eagle Wing, Little Bird's father, would accept no less than the fine horse he demanded. So Billy went to a Native American friend of his who provided him with a horse.

Once again alas, for the horse did not really belong to Billy's friend. Instead, it was the property of one Clement Bernard, who also yearned to wed Little Bird. Somehow learning about the situation, he showed up and claimed his horse. No bride for Billy.

Eagle Wing threw Billy out of the lodge. Young, impetuous and overcome with grief at the loss of his beloved, Billy put a gun to his head and ended his life on July 24, 1879.

Hearing about his brother's suicide, John went looking for the man who had deceived Billy by giving him a horse that did not belong to him. John also sought Bernard, intending to kill them both to avenge his brother's tragic death. When he entered the Indian agent's office, he found both men there; opening fire, he killed Bernard. Alas once more, for several of Bernard's friends were present. They immediately surrounded the killer, preparing to lynch him, but the Indian agent intervened and sent Billy to Camp Sheridan, where he was held under guard awaiting trial.

At length, the trial took place. In a curious turn of events—perhaps a reflection of the culture of frontier justice—John was acquitted of the crime. Watrous says he relocated to Michigan, "not troubled by regrets over avenging the untimely death of his brother."

History does not record whom Little Bird eventually married, or whether she married at all. We know from local newspaper reports that the elder John Provost was heartsick about the death of one son and the disappearance of another. "Love, jealousy and revenge," says Watrous, all played a part in bringing the Provost family such great sorrow.

A Hardy Pioneer

Hazel Ramsey was only twelve when her mother died, leaving her to care for her younger siblings in the unforgiving climate of Pingree Park, high up Poudre Canyon. In 1912, Frank Koenig came to the park and boarded with the Ramseys. The two fell in love, married and established their own homestead nearby. Frank ran the first telephone line to the park and transformed the trail from the canyon highway into the park into a drivable road.

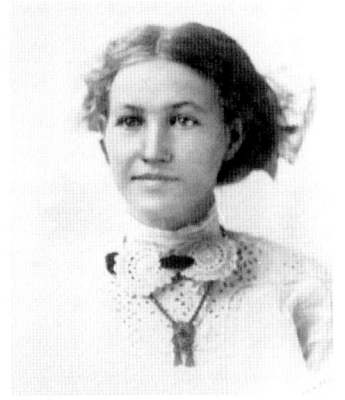

Hazel Koenig. *LHA H00490.*

Strangers on a Train

Stranded in the snow on Christmas—it could happen to anyone, even today. But this story takes place in 1878 and is about a young widow, her two small children and three men on a train. Author John Monett recounts a missionary's tale, told with no names but real nonetheless.

The Denver Special left Russell, Kansas, on the morning of December 24. The mother was going to live with her mother; her children were looking forward to a joyful celebration with their grandmother.

As the train chugged along through light snow, the three men, a salesman (a "drummer" back then), a well-to-do ranch owner and a weathered cowboy, heard the woman's story—her fruitless attempt to keep the farm going after her husband's death, her hopes to borrow $100 and open a small shop in Denver. After crossing into Colorado, the train encountered a full-blown blizzard, driven by fierce wind. Eventually it came to a full stop, huffing and puffing in the frigid air. The passengers would have to spend the night waiting for rescue.

Rescue appeared doubtful. No one had any way of contacting the outside world. An intrepid crew member set off into the storm, following the tracks as best he could, to reach a telegraph station, but who knew whether he would make it? The snow was blinding.

When the children heard that they would not get to their grandmother's house in time for Christmas, they began to cry, inconsolable. The men spread their coats along the hard seats to make the children a bed and then, after conferring, decided to provide a little Christmas. Santa, they told the children, would come after all. They should hang stockings. The girl protested—the only stockings she owned were on her feet. The rancher said he had a brand-new pair in his bag; they would do, and he assured the children the men would tell Santa the stockings were for the children. Thus comforted, they slept.

Off the men went to the baggage car, where they found many small gifts in the drummer's stash. Even the crew got in on the excitement, and everyone but the children stayed up all night. When morning came, the children found not only two stockings bulging with gifts but also a small sagebrush decorated with ribbons—a makeshift Christmas tree. They were overjoyed.

The train was finally rescued, for the crewman did reach his destination. A horse-drawn snow plow arrived, along with a cooked turkey to feast on. The train got to Denver under a clear sky late on Christmas Day. As the strangers on the train parted ways, the men gave the young woman a gift: an ornate photo album with signatures where their pictures would have been. Tucked in between the pages, the young widow found a $100 bill.

Houses and Hotels

Shotgun houses, one room wide and four rooms long, were inexpensive and common in the early years. To the right of this one on an alley off Mason Street, the original courthouse on Howes Street and Laporte Avenue is visible. Though the building has been rebuilt several times, the courthouse location has remained the same.

The Timnath Hotel, shown here, housed a drugstore and medical office operated by Dr. W.S. Partridge. Built in 1900, the two-story frame building later became a private home. During its days as a hotel, Mrs. Anna Williams was the proprietress. While it was the only hotel in Timnath, a small settlement east of town, Fort Collins had several hotels by the 1900s, including the Tedmon and the Northern.

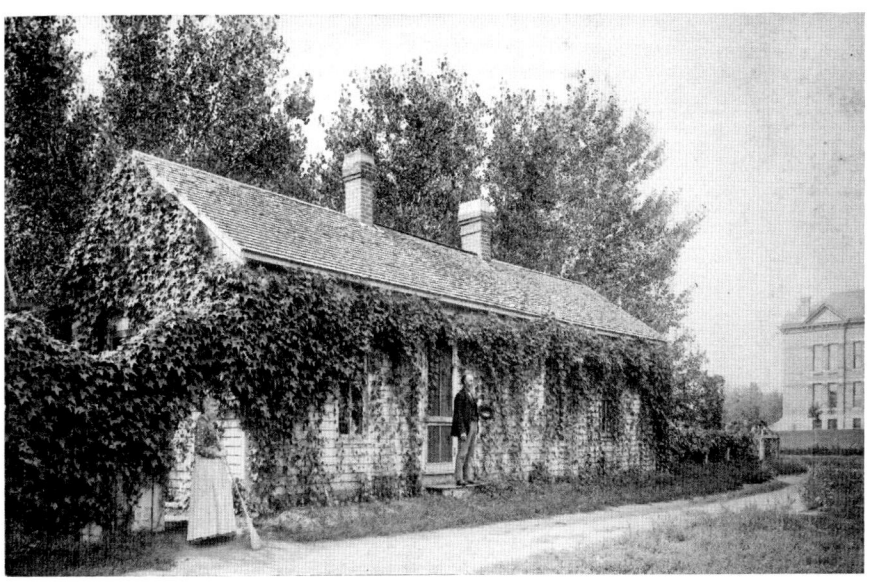

A shotgun house. *MEM.*

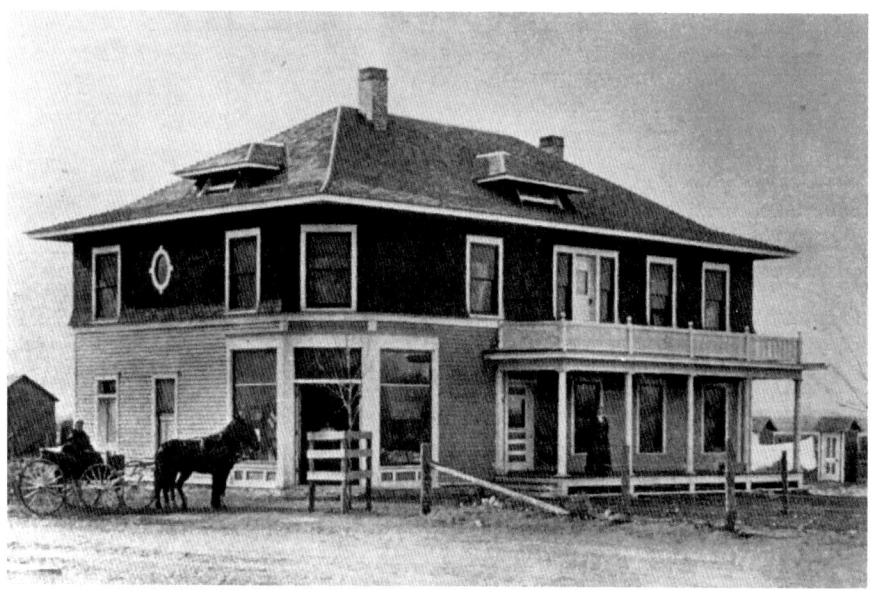

Timnath Hotel. *LHA H03761*.

Harmony

Almost 150 years ago, a small settlement a few miles south of Fort Collins formed a district and called it Harmony, in the expectation that the residents would live in peace with one another and in harmony with nature. In the early 1870s, people began farming there; one family farmed along what is now Timberline Road, living at first in a dugout on land once inhabited by Chief Friday Fitzpatrick and his Arapahos.

One early settler was Ben Preston, who came in 1869, before the district was even established, and had problems farming until he happened onto alfalfa, which proved to grow well in the climate and was welcomed as livestock feed. Preston, who could easily have given up and gone elsewhere, was yet another stubborn pioneer who refused to accept defeat and kept trying until he met with success.

More settlers came, and soon the colony had a school, built in 1878 and named Muddy School; a church; and a busy general store.

Around the turn of the century, Harmony acquired a train depot, a grain elevator and a sugar beet dump. The sugar beet industry was prosperous, growing in importance in this area, by 1900; a processing plant was built in Fort Collins a few years later.

In 1891, the settlers carved out a cemetery that has remained in the same place, the southwest corner of Harmony Road and McMurry Avenue, for more than a century, although no burials have taken place there since 1940. The headstones tell poignant stories of those early settlers. (A plaque on the fence labels it "Harmony Cemetary [sic].")

Watson and Martha Ziegler came to the area in 1895. A Seventh-day Adventist preacher, Ziegler served area churches along with farming the land. The farm did well; soon the family built a large brick home, the only residence still standing from that long-ago little town. In 1991, the building and land were donated to CASA (Court Appointed Special Advocates) for use as a safe place for parents and children to see one another during court-mandated separations. Today it is known as Harmony House, and Ziegler Road, which intersects with Harmony Road, recognizes the original owners of the land.

The Harmony School that stands at the northeast corner of Harmony and Timberline is the third incarnation of the old Muddy School. Built in 1931, named Harmony School and used for many years as a grammar school, it was acquired in 1978 by a private group that now operates a preschool on the premises.

In its day, Harmony had flourishing cherry and apple orchards. This author well remembers driving "out to Harmony" each fall to pick ripe fruit from the trees. The soil was rich and the yields were good. And the people were very neighborly; it was a harmonious place.

Farming the Land

Kenneth Thayer and Leona Baxter married in 1932, at the height of the Great Depression. Before their marriage, Leona earned a degree at the college and taught composition, science and bookkeeping; she even drove

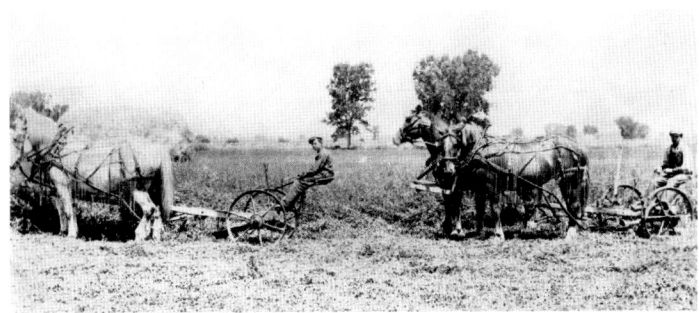

Kenneth Thayer, *left*, with Lady and Bridget. *MEM.*

a school bus. Like other farmland around Fort Collins, the Thayer farm has long since been absorbed into the city. Until the mid-twentieth century, the economy of Fort Collins was based on agriculture, supported by the land-grant college founded to improve farming and ranching practices. Like many other farmers then, Thayer still used horses on his farm.

Chapter 3
MEMORABLE PEOPLE

Everyone's life is a story. The vast majority of pioneers who settled the West lived out their lives in similar ways, with hard work and sacrifice, sorrow and loss, failure and success and a daily struggle to survive. While their stories were often passed down through the generations, many of these quiet lives faded into history to become part of the larger fabric of the frontier story.

But not all the stories were lost. Beyond the larger-than-life individuals mentioned in the introduction who colored our early history, beyond the town founders, many of whom are memorialized by Old Town street names, there were unique and notable people who left us their legacies in various ways. This chapter tells tales of intrepid frontier women, courageous and determined settlers and a rapscallion or two. Each one of them created a memorable connection to Fort Collins.

An Irish Immigrant

Given the way Americans live in the twenty-first century, it takes a great leap of the imagination to turn back the clock to the nineteenth century, when Fort Collins was a fledgling settlement on the edge of the high plains, teetering on the brink of extinction. Nature—drought, grasshoppers, blizzards and more—and economics had taken a severe toll, leaving a small band of hangers-on who envisioned a future they believed in.

After all, the town was along a beautiful river rich with fish in a lush valley teeming with wildlife and offering a mostly moderate climate. Surely it could—would—succeed.

Yet what courage, what determination and faith were required to see beyond the dark days to what lay beyond! The handful of hopefuls could so easily have given up and gone back to a more comfortable, safer, more prosperous life. Luckily for Fort Collins, they decided to stay. Today they are known as the founders of Fort Collins, as indeed they were. But who were they, really?

One outstanding founder was James Arthur, memorialized by the Arthur Ditch. Coming to Colorado in 1859 to search for gold, Arthur soon discovered the high value of hay, in those days much more lucrative than gold. With enterprise and energy, he set to work to harvest, dry and bale hay. He lived in a tent and bent his back to the task, using a scythe and rake. At that time, hay was baled with a box. Pitched in, tramped down and wrapped with rope, it was then ready for transport and sale.

Only one problem—Arthur found the boxes of hay too bulky to manage alone. So he and a partner, John Hahn, acquired an old cotton press and used it instead. According to a 1963 article in the *Coloradoan* newspaper, this was the first use of a cotton press for that purpose west of the Mississippi.

Prospering with his hay business, Arthur soon turned to livestock, driving a herd of cattle from Missouri to his farm. He was blessed with luck in this endeavor, and he ran his cattle ranch until the 1880s. By then well-to-do, he built a brick house on East Mulberry Street and subsequently became a county commissioner, state senator, bank president, city council member and mayor.

When he died in 1905, the *Fort Collins Courier* described him as "the most charming of men, genial, kind and obliging."

When James Arthur came to America from Ireland in 1849, at age fourteen, he first worked in a grocery store, then as a cabin boy on a steamship. Then adventure called him to the unknown West, and he answered unhesitatingly. Like so many other early settlers, once here he persevered, bringing integrity and progressive thinking to a small western outpost. For him as for other determined folks, giving up was simply not an option.

Captain Josiah McIntyre

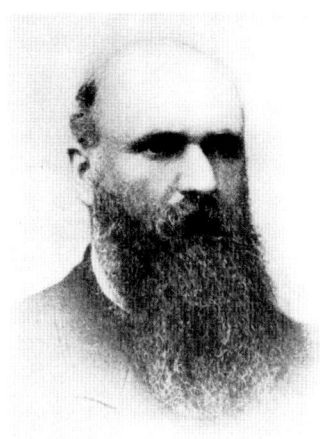

Josiah McIntyre. *LHA McInty_1.*

When the Civil War began, Josiah McIntyre joined the Sixteenth Pennsylvania Cavalry, rising in due time to the status of captain. (During the war that almost tore America asunder, militias were assembled within states, rather than by the federal government, and sometimes by individuals with the funds to arm the soldiers.) Leaving his new bride, Lucy, who parted from her young husband "with smiles instead of tears" because of "the great cause" for which he was fighting, as Ansel Watrous describes it, McIntyre went off to war.

Wounded most severely under his left eye at the Battle of Shepherdstown, Virginia, in September 1862 (the first time the 118th Pennsylvania had come under fire), McIntyre was taken prisoner, and his wounds were not treated skillfully. Even though he was exchanged soon after being captured and rejoined his regiment, he was discharged when his sight began to fail.

Undaunted, McIntyre went to Missouri, where he studied law and passed the bar, soon becoming county judge of Caldwell County. Just why he came to Fort Collins is unclear, but come he did, first to homestead and then to move into town to open a law practice. However, by 1885, he was completely blind. Still determined to complete his study of law, he went to the University of Michigan. His daughter Loa read his assignments to him and helped him with his studies. With only his memory and his keen intelligence, McIntyre learned what he needed to know, and in 1889, he graduated with high honors, becoming the first blind man in the United States to earn a law degree. Unfortunately, he did not live long to enjoy the fruits of his labors; he died in 1892.

But the hand of fate was not done with the McIntyre family. As a young adult, Loa went to Fort Duschene, Utah, to teach Ute Indians on a reservation there. She was so well respected and popular that the tribe adopted her. She married Harry Windsor and planned to settle with her husband in Utah. But in August 1900, this bright young woman with a promising future was killed on a hunting trip when a gun in the buggy she was riding in accidentally discharged. No one ever discovered how the weapon discharged or why. She was thirty years old. Her body was returned to Fort Collins for burial. This left only one of Josiah and Lucy's seven children, a son, Clyde.

Lucy Richards McIntyre survived her husband by many years and became a pillar of the community, working with the Woman's Christian Temperance Union, studying the Bible and serving as a staunch member of the Methodist Episcopal Church. She lived to be ninety-five, dying in 1940—while Fort Collins was still officially dry. Lucy's gravestone reads, "Faith, Hope, Love—The Last of the Crusaders."

Thus did these members of the McIntyre family become part of the rich, lively history of our town, each in his or her unique way.

Hard Choices

During the early years of settlement around this area, many single men who had ventured west married Native American women. One of them, E.W. Whitcomb, married an Oglala Lakota woman called Kate. (Her tribal name is unknown.)

Whitcomb may have been the first white settler in Boxelder Valley, coming here in 1867. He and his wife began their life together in a teepee near the fort. Whitcomb gradually became more prosperous, operating ranches from along the Poudre River to Chugwater, Wyoming, according to authors Arlene Ahlbrandt and Mary Hagen.

Kate mingled her native tongue, French and English in her speech. She was skilled at leather work, making clothing and moccasins for her family. Ahlbrandt and Hagen describe her as "a quiet person with a low, musical voice."

But in the 1870s, when Whitcomb decided to move to Cheyenne, Kate did not want to leave her people. Her husband packed up his belongings, gave her a horse and supplied her with necessities and departed for his new home. He was not the first husband to leave a wife behind, nor would he be the last, but looking back, historians can only ponder the reasons for his dogged determination to move north without his family. And speculate, too, at how his wife must have felt, having made her choice.

Yet that painful choice proved unwise. Her people told her that hunting was poor—game was hard to find—and that settlers were taking over the land; they were a tidal wave rolling westward, unstoppable. She would be better off, they told her, to return to her husband and learn the ways of the whites. Whitcomb had promised that he would help her adapt if she stayed with him.

So back she went, abandoning forever her tribal life and the culture she had known. Whitcomb was true to his word. He found a tutor to educate his family in how to dress; how to read, write and speak proper English; and how to behave in polite society. Kate mastered the art of entertaining guests in the mansion he built for them in Cheyenne. As the authors note, she certainly must have encountered discrimination, but her gracious manner eventually earned her acceptance within the Cheyenne social scene.

"Whick" (as she called him) continued with his ranching enterprises, though he suffered a severe setback during the blizzard of 1886–87, and historians do not know how his wife coped with leaving her early life behind. By the time their three daughters, Lizzie, Ida and May, had grown, the lives of Kate's people had altered dramatically. Struck by lightning while outdoors on his Wyoming ranch, Whitcomb died in June 1915 at the age of eighty-one. And Kate? History reveals no more.

Francis Carter-Cotton

Deceivers come in all guises—sweet-faced children, innocent-looking youths and, sometimes, an educated, dignified man such as Francis Carter-Cotton, who pulled a fast one on some local residents and got away with it.

An Englishman who came to America to seek his fortune—or perhaps adventure—Carter-Cotton first showed up in Fort Collins around 1877. He decided to devote his leadership abilities and energy to the problem of water for agriculture and accordingly purchased about 10,000 (or 100,000, depending on the source) acres for a new company, the North Fork Ditch Company. The plan was to draw water away from the river into canals and ditches, even though more than ninety other diversions were already in place.

By 1881, the company was underway. Carter-Cotton had a sizable, profitable cattle herd to sustain his business ventures, but as the digging progressed, it developed that two tunnels needed to complete the project were proving much more expensive than anticipated. Then the price of cattle fell, so Carter-Cotton began borrowing heavily from the Travelers Insurance Company in Hartford, Connecticut, and from local investors.

He sold several parcels to farmers, but that still did not alleviate his financial troubles.

Ansel Watrous appears to consider the entrepreneurial Englishman a solid citizen, for he depicts Carter-Cotton generously: president of the stock growers' association, provider of a hefty sweepstakes prize at a county fair and organizer of the 1884 county fair. Watrous notes that Carter-Cotton and Joseph Mason jointly owned a mercantile.

Curiously, Watrous bypasses the incident that left its mark on Fort Collins: on November 18, 1886, Carter-Cotton was confronted in his office by several local businessmen to whom he owed money. It appears that the Englishman, who had been well liked and considered a prominent citizen, had built up some level of trust, for he told the men he had to mail a letter and wanted to get it on the 3:00 p.m. train. Naïvely, they believed him (he had previously assured his creditors he would go to England to get the money)—until they heard a key turn in the office door lock and found themselves locked in.

Going out through the transom was the only possible escape route, as the office was on an upper floor, so one by one—after waiting some considerable time for their debtor to return—over they climbed (except one portly gentleman who, to his embarrassment, got stuck). They then learned that their prey, who left behind over $300,000 in debts, had boarded a Denver train to Kansas City, never to be seen in Fort Collins again.

But in time they had news: Carter-Cotton surfaced in British Columbia, where he refashioned himself as a respectable citizen, untouchable in the United States. Curses—foiled again.

Mrs. Dr. Miller

Born in Illinois in 1867, Nora Rice came in 1893 to Fort Collins, where she taught sixth and seventh grades at Franklin School. How she met the widowed Dr. Charles Perry Miller is lost to history, but meet him she did, and they soon married.

Dr. Charles Miller was one of the earlier settlers here. A physician, he served as county coroner in 1888 and in that position had to gather a jury to perform an inquest about a murder, that of Eva Howe, whose husband, James Howe, cut her throat in full view of the local citizenry. Onlookers watched in horror as the hapless victim bled to death. James was hanged by a mob in the dark of night.

Nora came west to teach, but when she married Dr. Miller, she became a homemaker and mother, as was the custom of the time. Women could teach if they were single or widowed but not if they were married; their role was to manage the home and care for the children.

Her husband's death of a heart attack in 1902 left her with two small daughters and no means of support. Although she had only the equivalent of a high school education, attained at a "normal school," Mrs. Miller was determined and undaunted. She gained admission to Michigan Medical School, an unusual accomplishment for a woman then, and spent almost two years there before transferring to the University of Colorado Medical School to receive her medical degree.

She had a tough row to hoe. Female doctors were more distrusted than trusted, so her practice was largely limited to maternity and pediatric care. Sometimes she drove long distances in her buggy—day or night, weather notwithstanding—to get to the home of a woman in labor. Fort Collins did have telephone service at that time, and Dr. Nora Miller surely had a telephone, but rural service was rare and expensive, so anxious husbands probably came to her Remington Street home to fetch her.

After practicing here for several years, Dr. Miller moved to southern Colorado, where she served as the only physician in Baca County and had a thriving practice for some time. During the Dust Bowl era, she moved to Texas, and during World War II, wanting to do her part, she returned to the schoolroom because teachers were so badly needed. Still a woman of science, she taught physics, mathematics and aeronautical science in Montana.

She continued teaching there and elsewhere until about 1949, according to Dr. Stanley Hensen's history of medicine in Fort Collins, and died ten years later at age eighty-one from heart failure. A grave memorial names her as "probably the first woman physician in Fort Collins," and her daughter, Mary Rice Wigle, called her "an awesome, gutsy lady." Indeed.

Another Gutsy Lady

"Granny" Edith Boothroyd regaled her grandson Jack Ogilvy with tales of her life on the American frontier. With her husband, Philip, she migrated west in 1874 to find herself, a seventeen-year-old British immigrant from an urban Victorian family, in the midst of the wild and woolly West, as foreign a land as she could have imagined. The couple first settled in

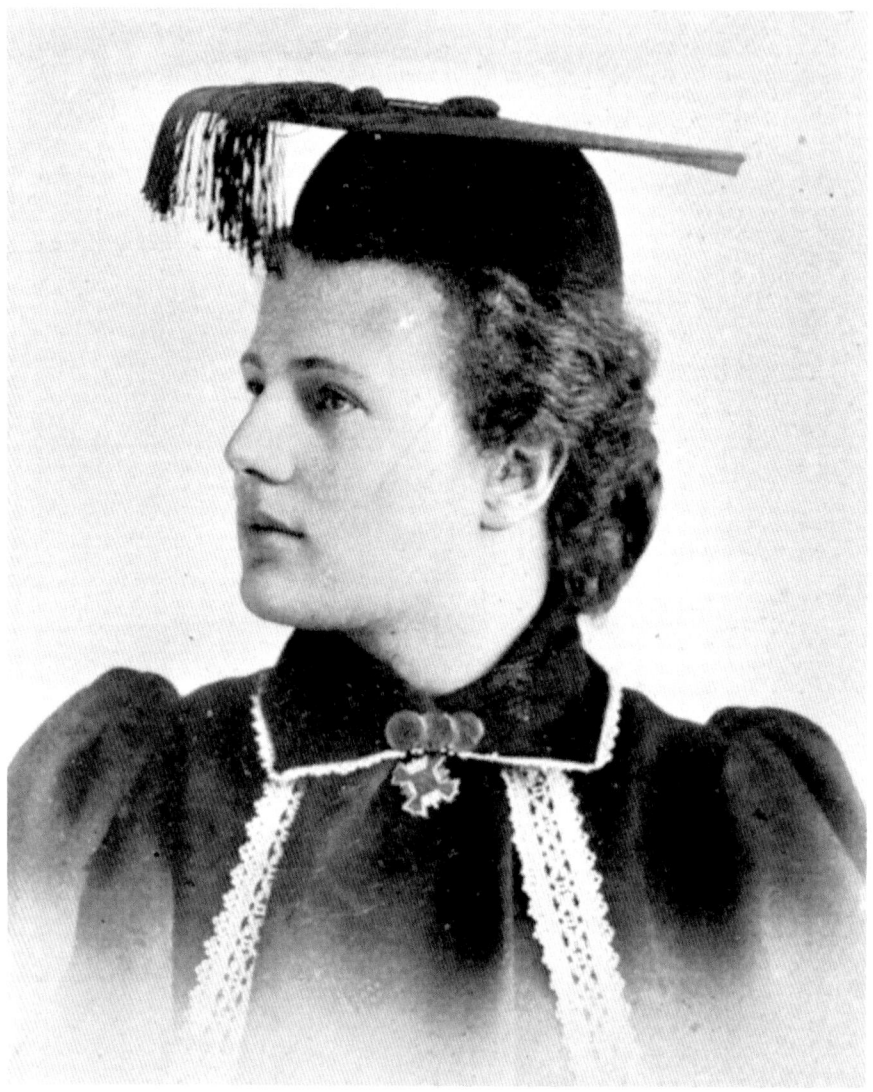

Edith M. Boothroyd's daughter, also named Edith, graduated from the agricultural college in 1892. *LHA B_throy.*

Spring Canyon west of Fort Collins, and Edith Boothroyd began her western adventure.

Ogilvy recalls that Boothroyd had to protect her delicate skin against the intensity of Colorado's high-altitude sun. She carried a parasol and wore veils when she went out. She soon acquired pets—a dog, a cat and a pig.

The pig, called Sairey Gamp, followed Boothroyd everywhere she went, even into town.

The English transplant could hold her own. She learned to handle horses, helped deliver babies and once scared off a mountain lion to protect her children. Still, there were moments when her inbred good manners were severely tested. When she first met mountain man Mariano Modena, he declared that it was time for a toast to the bride. Picking up some dusty wine glasses, he ran his finger around the edges and poured the libation. Boothroyd drank and returned the toast, managing to contain her startled reaction to his manners, to which she was so unaccustomed. However, when he handed her what looked like a collection of horsehair, which she discovered was actually scalps, she found it very difficult to maintain her composure.

Ogilvy's Granny nursed the sick as pioneer women often did. She learned to cook and do laundry and keep the home going in the manner of her time, all while caring for her children as they came along.

Heading home one evening at dusk, she started to cross over a rickety bridge when it gave way, dropping the back legs of one of her mares through the opening. She was alone; dark was gathering. What to do? What else but "keep calm and carry on"? Which she did, somehow managing to calm the second horse, unhook the team and lead the untangled horse off the bridge, find enough small rocks to construct a ramp under the trapped mare's hind legs, coax the horse to step up the ramp and then over the bridge, tie the mare with her companion, go back for the wagon and drag it across the bridge, hook up her team again and head home.

"That," says her nephew John Glass, "was one of the most incredible feats of horsemanship I've ever heard of."

Summing up, the authors of *Hardship and Hope* say, "If history should ever again pit a refined English gentlewoman against a wild and vast frontier, knowing 'Granny' we'll place our bets on the lady."

THE DICKERSON SISTERS

They were born about a year apart, in 1910 and 1911, into the mountain life, and by choice they never left it. Helen and Alice Dickerson, two indomitable sisters who never married, lived out their long lives in Buckhorn Canyon.

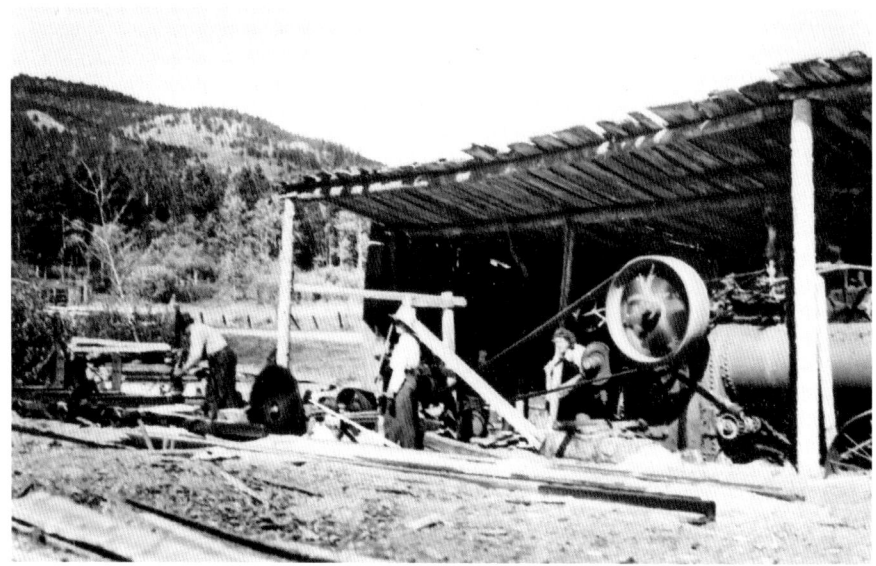

From left: Allen, Alice and Helen Dickerson at the sawmill, circa 1950s. *LHA H08354.*

At age four, Helen led a horse working to clear land for planting. This was no hardship to her; it was a normal part of both girls' childhood. Always, there was hard work to do, and they did it.

Their grandfather Sam Dickerson had come to Eaton, Colorado, at the urging of his uncle Benjamin Eaton, former governor of Colorado, where Sam's son Earl was born. In Eaton, Earl met Stella Foster, in Colorado seeking relief from asthma, and the two married. Not long after their first child, Helen, was born, they moved to Buckhorn Canyon. The log cabin they lived in housed extended family—and the two sisters for all their long lives.

Since the cabin had no electricity or running water and was heated by a wood stove, mere survival took considerable time—chopping wood, drawing water, caring for livestock and more. The sisters knew no other way of life; only late in life did they acquire running water. Just making a living was equally daunting. The family logged wood and sold fence posts and poles made at their sawmill. After their father's death in 1942, the two women had a large order of bridge planks to fill for the forest service. Though small in stature, the sisters were large in courage and determination. They filled the order.

Throughout their lifetimes, they knew hardship, lean times, sorrow and loss. When Earl had a heart attack, Alice drove him to a hospital; on the way, they were hit head-on by another car, and their father died in her arms. From then on, Alice was a reluctant driver at best. Both crack shots, they felt relatively safe in their isolated home, but once two men forced their way in, tied them up and demanded money before either of the women could get off a shot. Another time, Alice shot an intruding bear in the nose to scare it off. It left.

As children, they had attended school off and on in Masonville, but a massive flood in 1923 trapped the family in the canyon for two years while roads were rebuilt—at times with only turnips to eat—so the rest of their education was in the school of hard knocks, as they liked to say.

As adults, they sold woven baskets, bolo ties, paintings and rag rugs at a small roadside stand to make ends meet. Their lively lives were filled with much more than can be recounted here. After Helen's death in 1992, at age eighty-two, Alice went on an African safari. She died in 1997, at age eighty-six. Though their cabin is gone, both women are canyon legends, much loved and long remembered.

The Strange Tale of Billy Batterson

Billy Batterson, son of pioneer settlers in the Livermore area, became a successful rancher with a large herd of cattle. He married Lilly Tibbetts, whose family had homesteaded nearby, and they had one son, William.

Elizabeth St. Clair operated the Log Cabin Hotel in the area. For reasons yet unknown, her son, Will, left the hotel and decided to move in with the Battersons. According to the Livermore Women's Club book *Among These Hills*, Will St. Clair was considered untrustworthy, even dangerous, by Billy's parents, by some neighbors and by Lady Catherine Moon, another neighbor.

But Billy seems to have considered him a friend. In 1908, Billy faced trial in Denver for possessing land illegally and was exonerated by St. Clair's testimony. However, a romance might have been brewing between St. Clair and Billy's wife—under Billy's nose. In 1908, Billy, fifty-five, became quite ill and was given eggnog as a remedy, causing violent stomach pains. St. Clair and Mary prevented Billy's father, Solomon Batterson, from seeing his son. The doctor arrived too late to save Billy. A subsequent autopsy was inconclusive as to whether his stomach contained any toxic substances, so no charges were brought even though Solomon and his wife, Mary, were convinced that their son had been poisoned by Lilly and St. Clair.

Right after Billy's death, St. Clair began spending large sums of money. Lilly insisted the money was back wages. After the funeral, St. Clair loaded Billy's body onto a wagon to take the coffin to the Livermore cemetery for burial. Along the way, a passerby reported seeing him sitting on the coffin, claiming that he had Billy Batterson right where he wanted him.

St. Clair's brushes with the law were not over. In 1909, he and Lady Catherine Moon's foster son, Frank Potts, were jailed in Denver for robbing a train. The two were eventually acquitted largely due to Lady Moon's efforts on behalf of Potts.

Lilly vigorously defended St. Clair, and he, in turn, defended her against accusations that she had been the cause of her husband's death. With her young son, William, she moved to Fort Collins, often going to Livermore to visit her mother, Frances Aldrich, and her sister, Mary Aldrich. St. Clair continued to manage the Batterson ranch.

Not long after Billy Batterson's mother died in 1910, Lilly and St. Clair were married. The marriage lasted twenty-seven years, even surviving another scrape with the law when St. Clair, accused of assaulting a sixteen-year-old girl and deciding the easiest choice was to marry her (even though he was already married to Lilly), was apprehended for bigamy. Not acquitted this time, he served a term in prison.

Perhaps today's forensic techniques would have solved the mystery of Billy Batterson's death, but in the early twentieth century, such tools were not at hand, so the mystery lingers on.

Music Maker

A local blacksmith, recalled only as "Dad" Morton and pictured on the following page in 1932, plied his trade during the daytime and played his fiddle at night. During the Great Depression, many farmers still used horses to plow their fields because tractors were too expensive, so his skills remained in demand, as were his nimble fingers to accompany square-dance callers. For a good many years, square dancing, born in barns across the frontier in the nineteenth century, dominated social life in rural America.

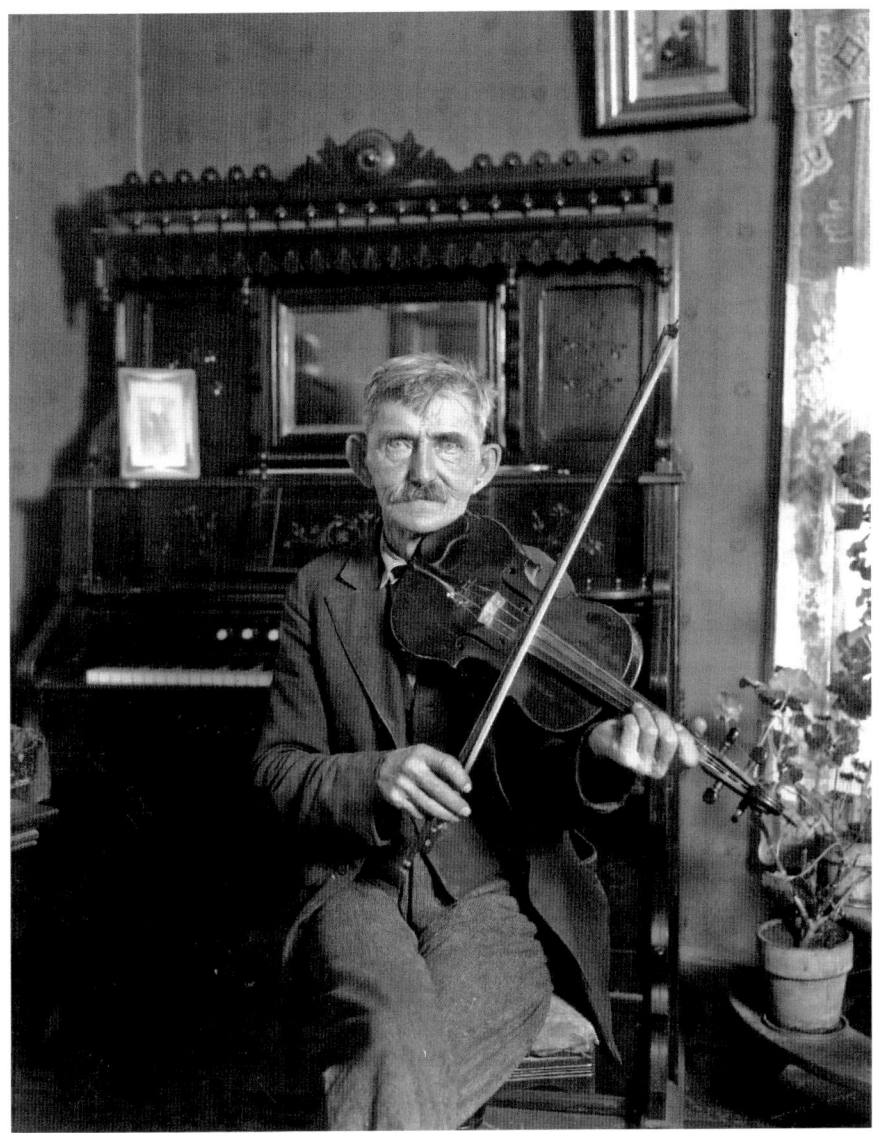

Fiddler "Dad" Morton. *MEM.*

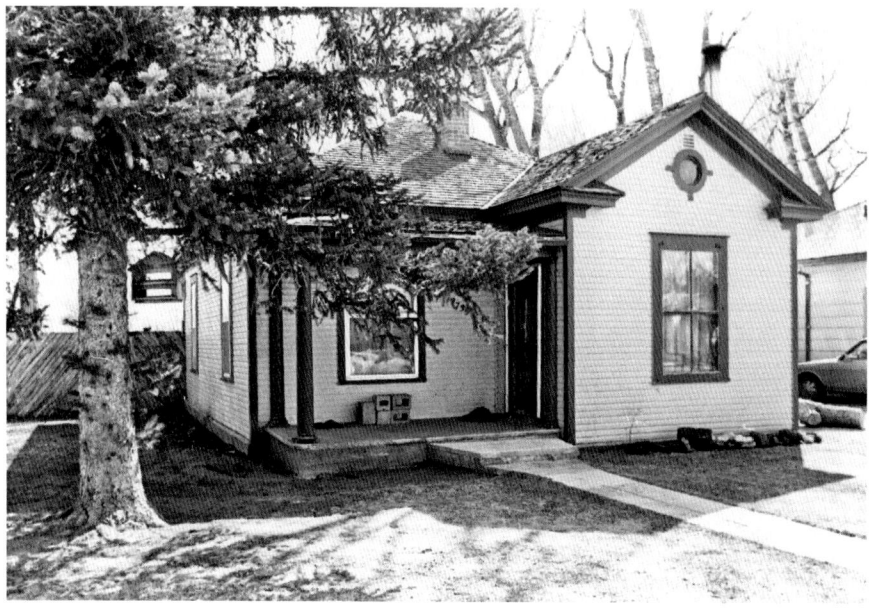

Byron White's Wellington home. *MEM.*

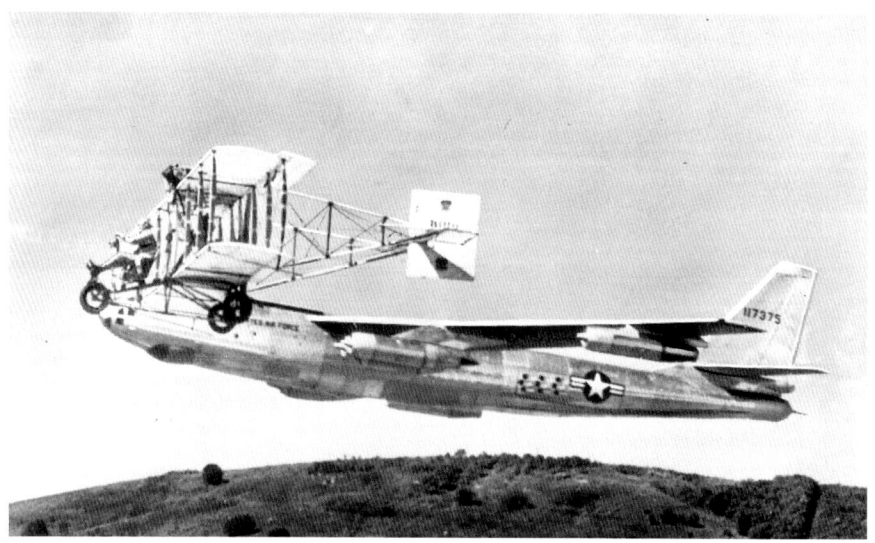

Billy Parker's biplane. *MEM.*

Native Sons

John F. Kennedy and Byron White met in England in 1939. White, whose childhood home is shown on the facing page, served in the navy during World War II, was valedictorian of his college class and played professional football before being named to the Supreme Court in 1962, after his friend John Kennedy became president in 1961. A moderate, White served for three decades.

Aviation had come a long way when this photograph was taken, circa 1953. A B-47, which could fly for many miles at 794 miles per hour, is shown with a 1912 pusher plane owned by Fort Collins transplant Billy Parker, who built his first biplane in a Fort Collins field in 1915. The airplane pictured could only stay airborne for ninety minutes, but his early biplanes led to a long, successful career in aviation.

The Songbird

Fort Collins native Ruth Burnett, daughter of prominent local citizen Frank Burnett, started singing and playing the piano when she was very young. She studied ballet and later went on to choreograph dances. As a teenager, she tried out for a role in Gilbert and Sullivan's *HMS Pinafore* in Denver, winning the lead role. She attended Fort Collins High School and graduated from high school in Phoenix, Arizona, where one of her classmates was politician Barry Goldwater.

She studied at the Arizona Conservatory of Music, mastering several languages in song, and later continued her studies at the University of Denver and the University of Colorado. She performed at the Orpheum Theater in Phoenix and at a Biltmore hotel opening there in 1926. Though she traveled to perform, she turned down an offer from George M. Cohan to go to New York City. With her husband, Lynn William Rice, she had one son, William; after her husband's death, she married Denver magnate Robert McDonald.

During the Great Depression in the 1930s, it was challenging at best to make a living in the music world (even the Metropolitan Opera Company went bankrupt), so Ruth took up modeling, working for Gano Downs and Daniels and Fisher department stores in Denver and taking part in style shows for clubs and organizations, including at the Brown Palace Hotel for the Denver Press Club. She continued to sing as well, performing for the Denver Opera Company and in numerous concerts and operas, among them *Madam Butterfly*, *Rigoletto* and *Carmen*. She also had lead roles in several light operas.

In the 1950s, she frequently performed at Shriner hospitals throughout the country, a connection brought about because her husband was a member of a Masonic order. She also devoted considerable energy to aiding handicapped children through music. An early advocate for the healing powers of music therapy, she believed that singing is healthy and music is therapeutic.

She did not retire from music when she returned to Fort Collins; rather, she gave singing lessons and promoted galas, which were musical evenings that raised funds for scholarships. Galas she directed were held at the Lincoln Center and at Rocky Mountain High School in the 1970s. Fort Collins pianist and Colorado State University professor Wendell Diebel produced both events.

Like her father—at eighty-seven, he wrote a book, *Golden Memories of Colorado*—McDonald enjoyed a long life. In her eighties, she continued to live a full, engaged life, traveling extensively, still steeped in music. As author Arlene Ahlbrandt commented in a newspaper article, "Music [was] her life." Born in 1905, McDonald lived to be almost one hundred, dying at ninety-nine in 2005, having lived an exemplary life enriched by the joys and rewards of making music and sharing it with others.

Chapter 4

LAW, ORDER AND PUBLIC SAFETY

Contrary to Hollywood's imaginings, the early West was not a lawless place, the scene of frequent shootouts in the streets, vigilante hangings or poker games in saloons that ended in gunplay with someone dead on the floor. Such things did happen from time to time, and in some towns maintaining law and order was a challenge at best. But there were laws, and there were enforcers of laws. Federal marshals were present in some areas; most towns had at least a sheriff and probably a deputy or two, and most towns had a jail, a duly elected judge and mainly law-abiding citizens. Lawlessness was more prevalent on open land, where outlaws rustled cattle, cattle men and sheep men waged war, officers of the law were seldom around and most homesteaders (including women) had weapons and knew how to use them. Moreover, they would not hesitate to do so if they felt threatened.

The most famous—or infamous—murder in Fort Collins happened in 1888 when James Howe came home very inebriated to find his wife, Eva, packing to leave him. After killing his wife, he was apprehended, dragged out of jail by a mob and hanged from a derrick at the under-construction courthouse, the only hanging in Fort Collins history.

Though that was perhaps the most dramatic law-and-order incident, other episodes made sure that the keepers of the peace were well occupied, especially during the time before prohibition (which started in 1896) was in place here. There were troublesome spots, particularly the quarry at Stout and "the jungle," the area around the Great Western Sugar Factory.

Fort Collins had its share of bootlegging after prohibition went into effect here and houses of ill repute as well. In one instance, when a dwelling of that nature burned down, the proprietress claimed it was arson; it may have been.

On the other hand, Fort Collins had an abundance of churches, and the majority of the residents here were upright, hardworking people. Still, local history records murders along with other illegal acts. This chapter recounts some stories of law and order, Fort Collins style.

Jailbreak

In 1864, Larimer County built a new jail in Laporte, then the county seat, at a cost of $150. John Mathews, county clerk and justice of the peace (for whom Mathews Street is named), was designated to oversee management of the jail. Soon afterward, Squire Mathews, as he was known, saw his first two prisoners delivered to the jail, locked in the small cell and settled down for a quiet night. The jail was a small log cabin, not quite as impermeable as one might wish a jail to be. The prisoners were due to be tried in district court and could not make bail. Mathews went to bed.

The two men, named "Red" and "Slim" in a later account (Watrous does not give their real names), were known to be horse thieves, a hanging offense, of a wily sort who knew how to evade justice. Red had hidden a knife on his person when they were apprehended, and it was not found after they were arrested. As soon as they were alone in the cell, Red began working away with the knife at the soft wood in the bottom of the frame that held the bars on the window in place. It didn't take long for the wood to give and not much longer—though no doubt a good deal of effort—for them to pull a bar out of the window. With one bar out, the men decided they could squeeze through.

Pulling and twisting, they managed to make their way out of the window via the slender opening. Slim, aptly named it would appear, got out more easily than Red, who was a bit heavier, but they both escaped from the jail without waking their jailer.

And there stood Mathews's horse in a stall, nearby and available. Quickly, quietly, they saddled the mare, jumped on her back and rode off into the night just before the break of dawn. Mathews slept through it all.

In the morning when he woke up, Mathews discovered his mount, saddle and all, gone along with his two prisoners. He found only the whittled wood and the broken bar. The horse, which belonged to the county, according to Watrous, was never seen again, nor were the two horse thieves, who presumably had the common sense to vacate the region for good.

Mathews's friends, says Watrous, never let him forget the daring deed that happened right under his nose, so to speak. When the county seat was moved to Fort Collins a few years later, so was the jail, housed in sturdy Old Grout, one of the original buildings at the fort—a structure much less vulnerable to clever, determined horse thieves.

Prohibition in Fort Collins

The situation was dire: saloons on every corner, drunken men staggering around, an increase in crime and James Shaw's death of exposure when he lay down on the sidewalk, inebriated, and froze to death. Something had to be done.

Pressured by the Woman's Christian Temperance Union (WCTU), led by Auntie Elizabeth Stone, the city passed an ordinance prohibiting the sale of liquor in 1873. Alas for the ladies, the ordinance was repealed only two years later when a group of businessmen petitioned the city fathers. There followed various unsuccessful attempts to stem the tide of "idle and vicious men" roaming the streets in their cups—an increase in the cost of a liquor license, which had been quite low (an unpopular move), for one. But the ladies persisted, even after Auntie Stone died, and in 1896, Ordinance 8 was passed, prohibiting the purchase, sale or providing by gift of liquor within the city limits. Perhaps impressed by the ordinance, Carrie Nation came here in 1906.

Creative businessmen and others found ways around the ordinance. In drugstores, liquor was sold under the guise of "medicinal purposes," and a brisk bootlegging business emerged. One memorable turn-of-the-century bootlegger was R.A. "Blackie" Mason. Until the quarry at Stout west of town shut down, the free-flowing supply of liquor drew locals, as did "the jungle" north of town, where crime was rampant. In the early twentieth century, Marie Lafitte was well known as an illicit source of liquor.

Driving to nearby Wellington, where there was a still, people sometimes got into accidents on the way home; moreover, revenue was leaving the city. It became increasingly clear that the ordinance needed to be eased a bit, so in 1936, the council approved the sale of 3.2 percent beer. Soon afterward, the Town Pump opened for business.

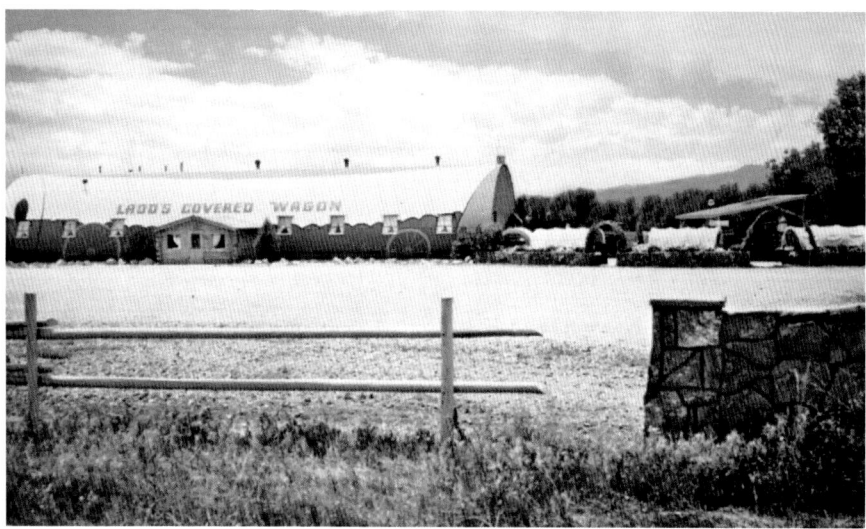

Ladd's Covered Wagon. *MEM.*

That did not answer the desire for hard liquor. In the 1950s, Justice of the Peace Wally Bujack recalled, officials were well aware of Boston Charlie, who sold liquor from the back of his taxicab but never got caught.

Ladd's Covered Wagon, just outside the city limits, was the first restaurant in the Fort Collins area to sell liquor to patrons. A converted Quonset hut, the restaurant was opened by Daisy and Lloyd Ladd in 1948 just a mile north of the city limits. After a two-year effort to obtain a license, the couple could legally sell patrons mixed drinks. In 1965, as the building was about to be sold, fire consumed the entire interior.

The WCTU remained active for a time, but the town was growing and changing. An influx of veterans after World War II, coming here to attend college on the GI Bill, meant a significant increase in population and sophistication. Under the leadership of William Morgan, Colorado A&M College became Colorado State University, expanding offerings and departments and drawing even more students. Industries like Woodward Governor came to town. The days of even semi-enforceable prohibition were clearly coming to an end.

So in the late 1960s, Mayor Tom Bennett gave up his position in order to join the city council and work for an end to prohibition, which had long since ended in the rest of the country. The effort was successful; in 1969, Ordinance 8 was repealed. After more than eighty years, Fort Collins was dry no longer.

WHO KILLED JOSEPH ALLEN?

Officer Joseph Allen, a relatively young man who was said to have connections in "the jungle," an unincorporated area surrounding the sugar beet factory, was murdered in 1907 by an unknown assailant. The case is still listed as an unsolved murder by the Fort Collins Police Department.

"The jungle" was known to have problems with crime. Because it was outside city limits, liquor was available there in what were known as dives. Allen, who was said to have had a wife and family in Kansas, had come to Fort Collins on a bicycle, according to historian Rose Brinks, and found a job in the police department. He liked to say that he knew people in "the jungle" and could deal with problems there. Unfortunately, on the night of July 3, his luck ran out.

Allen was ambushed as he strolled along on his beat. There were numerous large cottonwood trees in the area at that time, and his attacker evidently concealed himself behind one or behind some bushes, jumping out to attack Allen. There is evidence that Allen tried to defend himself, but the assault was so sudden and unexpected that he could not. He was hit in the head repeatedly, probably with a brick. Moaning and unconscious when found, he died at the hospital a few hours later.

One newspaper account indicates that Allen had once been a Pinkerton man, serving with the detective agency founded just before the Civil War. He later served in the army in Cuba and the Philippines. He was only in his late forties when he was killed.

Shortly before the murder, a doctor making a house call nearby reported having seen Allen talking with one of the men later arrested; however, they appeared to be having a friendly conversation, with no evidence of anger between them. This sighting took place about an hour before the murder in the exact spot where the attack happened.

A jury was empaneled to investigate the incident and determined, after viewing the body, that Allen had died from several blows to the head.

Although the police appealed to the public to help solve this shocking crime, and two men were subsequently arrested, no charges were brought and no one came forward with information. The murder appeared to have been planned, for it was known that Allen did his rounds nightly in that area. Allen's revolver, club and knife had been taken by the murderer.

City officials, businessmen and citizens were aroused and angered by the murder, some vowing to get rid of "the jungle," called by newspapers "a plague spot," altogether. Others were deeply concerned about the city's reputation as a law-abiding community. In time, the area changed, and other events diverted attention. Most people forgot, after a while. But the police have not forgotten—a street near the Timberline police station bears his name, and the case remains open.

Shot by the Sheriff

Numerous witnesses had told city marshal William Richart that Robert Miller was bottling liquor, which was illegal in Fort Collins at that time, and warrants had been sworn out for Miller's arrest. On a Saturday afternoon in May 1903, Richart entered the establishment, accompanied by deputies—all armed, in case of trouble.

There was trouble.

The men found Miller's son, young George Miller, in the front by the counter. He told them his father was in the back room. As they entered the darkened room, they saw Miller standing by the door warning them not to go in. Although he was told they had warrants to search the property and for his arrest, Miller resisted. Words were exchanged, and despite conflicting testimony at the trial, no one disputed that some scuffling took place.

The sequence of events gets murky here. According to testimony recorded in the newspaper, one of the men accompanying Richart took out his gun and pointed it at George. Richart took out his own weapon. Miller reportedly said, "To hell with your gun; we are not afraid of it" and picked up a bottle, preparing to throw it. He threw the bottle, Richart fired and Miller went down, shot in the chest. Richart was charged with murder.

During the trial, Richart maintained that he had tried to stop Miller and that the bottle coming toward him was heavy and looked full, a "dark-colored beer bottle." He said that when he saw Miller reaching under the counter, he thought he was getting a revolver. Hit by the bottle, the marshal sustained a head injury, which aided in his defense. Witnesses also said that George had picked up a club to defend his father.

By this time, George's brother John had returned to the store. One of the deputies told the brothers to leave the premises, encouraging them with his revolver, so they would not have to see their father's dead body, but George had been nearby when his father was shot and continued to insist that Richart fired as his father was throwing the bottle and that the bottle he threw did not have much liquid in it.

The county coroner testified that the wound on Miller's head was probably incurred when he fell and landed on pieces of broken glass rather than being inflicted by Richart or one of his men.

Trials happened more swiftly in those days; not long after the shooting, a jury of six men was empaneled (women were not allowed to serve on juries here until the late 1940s). They deliberated over the weekend and came back on Monday morning with a verdict of not guilty, judging the shooting accidental and therefore not a crime.

Tragic Tales

In October 1908, two powder men placed a dynamite charge that failed to ignite. One of the men went to check on the charge, resulting in a fatal explosion at the Ingleside limestone quarry in Owl Canyon north of Fort Collins. Seven workers were killed and fourteen injured.

In the 1920s, Fort Collins citizens were in a frenzy after the discovery of oil near Wellington. Investors envisioned riches beyond imagining. But in 1924, when a fire at the Mitchell oil well burned unchecked for over a month, the excitement paled. No one knew how to extinguish an oil fire. Firefighters donned asbestos suits to protect themselves from the fierce

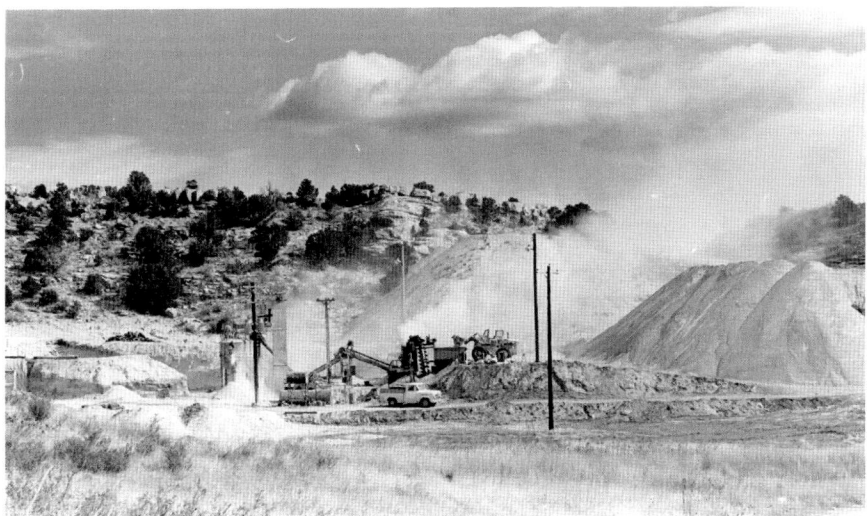

Ingleside Quarry. *LHA H09906.*

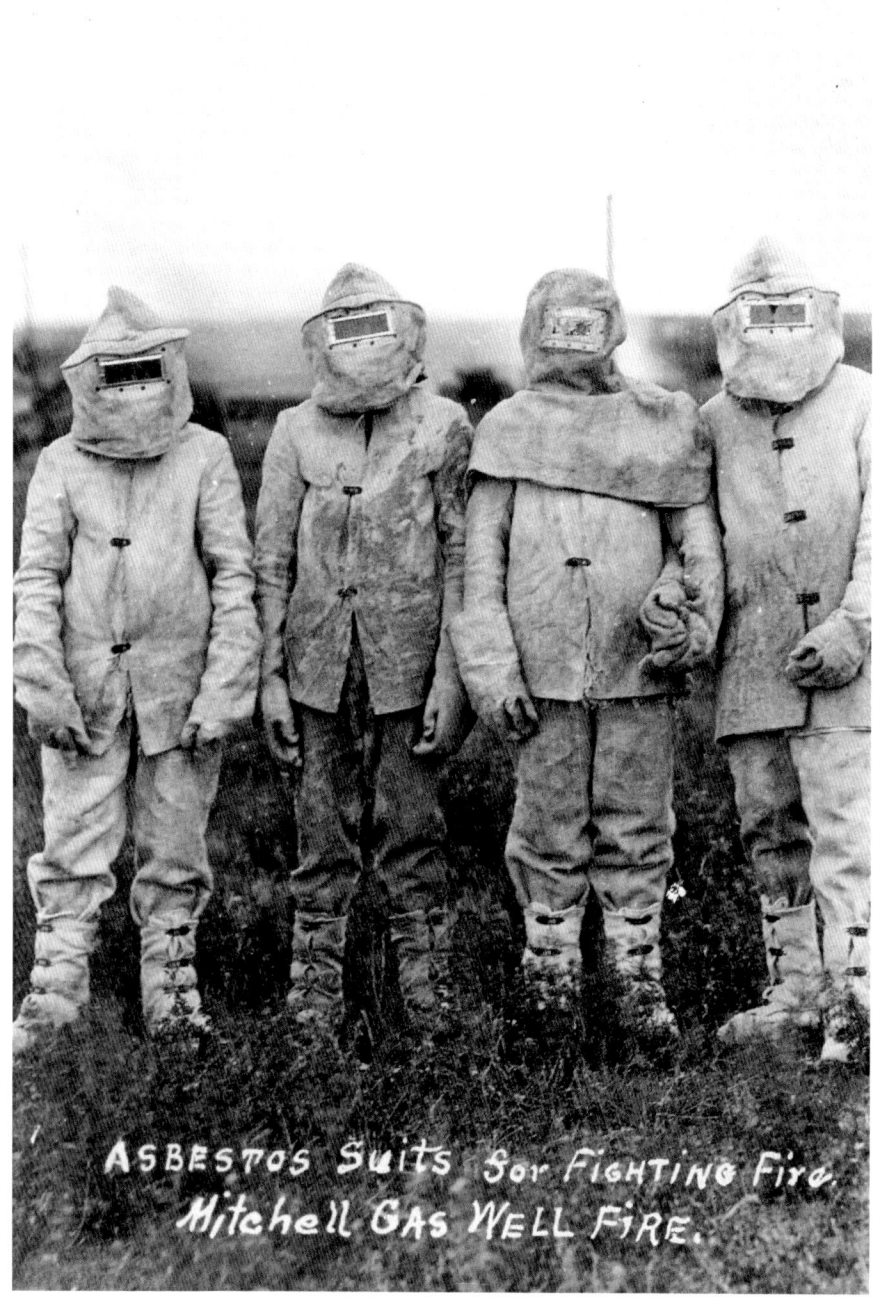

Asbestos firefighting suits. *MEM.*

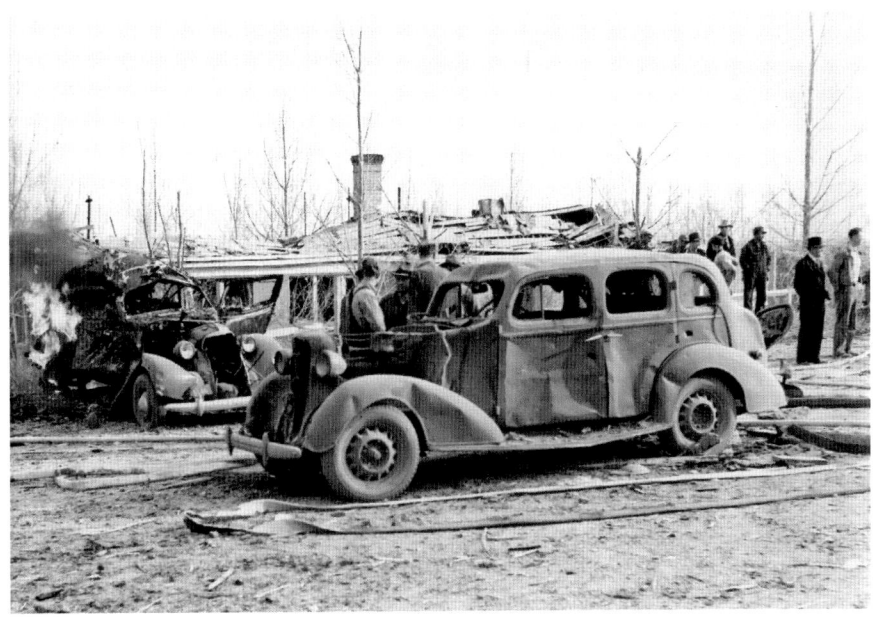

Ideal Cement explosion. *MEM*.

flames. In this time before OSHA, unprotected spectators lined up every day to see the spectacle.

On January 31, 1939, two workers at Ideal Cement in Laporte were killed and several others injured when three truckloads of dynamite exploded. Reverberations were felt as far away as Fort Collins; some nearby buildings were damaged. The plant operated, with a better safety record, under several different owners until 2004.

The Trial of William Town

Local sentiment was against William Town, who had been arrested for killing William Gardner, a respected family man well liked in Laporte. Shortly after the arrest, a lynch mob gathered. "The rope and the tree were ready," reported the *Weekly Courier*. But Deputy Sheriff William Richart, warned of the situation, diverted his prisoner away from Laporte until the mob cooled off.

Premeditated murder or self-defense? That's what the jury had to decide. William "Toughy" Town confessed to fatally shooting William Gardner when both were inebriated. Town and Gardner, workers at the Stout quarry west of town, had been drinking heavily on the afternoon of February 9, 1904. Claiming it wasn't loaded, Gardner brandished a pistol, which Town somehow took from him. Gardner stepped outside to retrieve his weapon. Town's father, Curtis Town, turned a gun on Gardner and told him to put his hands up. Gardner complied. Young William appeared with a Winchester rifle, which he pointed at Gardner, who said, "Don't shoot."

Barbara Rims, mother of quarry supervisor Thomas Griffith, echoed Gardner's plea. But Town ignored her and fired several times, hitting Gardner in the lung. Three hours later, Gardner died of his wounds. On the advice of his father, Town reported the crime, apparently believing he had nothing to fear, and was arrested. Several witnesses to the shooting confirmed this sequence of events.

What became fuzzy were the details. One witness asserted that Gardner had insulted the women in the cabin. Another said Town had threatened to shoot the elderly Mrs. Rims. One maintained that Mrs. Griffith, wife of the quarry supervisor, had behaved immorally, a charge she emphatically denied.

Evidence against Town continued to mount. One witness said Town had provoked a fight because he'd been dismissed from the quarry, even though he'd later returned to work. But the most damaging testimony came from eleven-year-old Lettie Griffith, who explained that she would never lie because if she did, she knew she would "burn in hell." She reported seeing Town ruthlessly shoot an *unarmed* man, a key issue for the jury.

When William Town took the stand, women were cleared from the courtroom, his testimony deemed unfit for their tender ears. Town claimed that Gardner had used foul language and hit him with a bottle—or was it a club? He had been too drunk to recall clearly. He said Gardner had grabbed him by the throat; he had to defend himself. However, several people had seen Curtis Town hold Gardner at gunpoint until his son had his Winchester rifle in hand, thereby contradicting Town's self-defense claim.

On March 16, the jury returned its verdict: guilty of first-degree murder. Reported the *Courier*, the jury first went 7–5 for hanging and then decided on life in prison. Town appeared relieved, preferring the "gloomy walls of the penitentiary" to the "trap and black cap, pinioned arms and legs. Hardened by crime as the young man is, yet he loves life." That "crime-hardened" lad was eighteen years old.

Murder of Newton Crose

"To young men in general, I would say don't drink. You never know what it will lead to." With those regretful words, William L. "Pat" Ryan accepted his conviction and sentence for the murder of attorney Newton Crose, a tragic event that took place more than one hundred years ago.

Crose was married to Franklin and Sara Avery's daughter, Marietta "Mettie" Louise, and had a thriving law practice. Unfortunately, he ran afoul of Ryan when Ryan's wife, the popular socialite Georgia Ott Ryan, filed for divorce (not easily obtained then) and Crose took her case.

Ryan, son of wealthy pioneer John L. Ryan, inherited his father's land and fortune in 1899 and appears to have enjoyed having money to buy racehorses (perhaps financed by selling off bits of land) and living the good life. The reason his wife sought the divorce is not known, but clearly Ryan was unhappy about it. On August 14, 1914, he charged into Crose's office in the Avery building, shot him twice and then followed him to a nearby doctor's office, where he shot him again. Occupants of another office, hearing the shots, captured the killer. Crose, who was only thirty-seven years old, died a short while later.

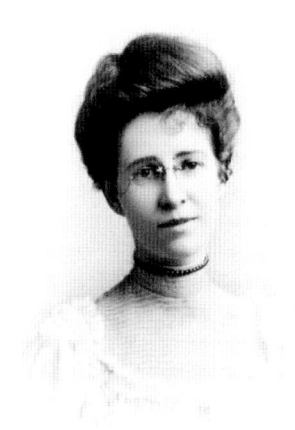

Marietta Crose, unexpected widow of attorney Newton Crose. *LHA H11562.*

Crose was an upstanding citizen of Fort Collins known to have read and studied Plato and was also an art aficionado. His death angered the community. Consequently, Ryan was swiftly brought to trial, found guilty and sentenced to be hanged. However, the following year, the Colorado Supreme Court determined that the first trial had been marred by incorrect instructions to the jury and an improper statement by the prosecutor that the insanity defense was "a disgrace to American jurisprudence," as quoted in the *Weekly Courier* newspaper.

At the second trial, Ryan was again found guilty, but his sentence was commuted to life in prison. He admitted his guilt but blamed his actions on being driven to desperation—his home broken up, his children taken from him. Whiskey, he said, was at fault for the killing. Misery and desolation followed the dissolution of his family, he claimed, and he could not help himself. While not denying his guilt, he did endeavor to rationalize what he had done. There were, in his eyes, extenuating circumstances.

Crose, of course, had done nothing more than his job, advocating to the best of his ability for his client, while Ryan had left the boundaries of the dry town he lived in to find ample supplies of liquor to fuel his anger and despair. Both men left bereaved families, as Crose went to his grave and Ryan went to prison. Before his departure from the courtroom, in an ironic twist, Ryan, murderer of an attorney, thanked his own attorney for saving his life.

The Trial of Harvey Miller

"But Mr. Sarchet, how can they prosecute me if I'm innocent?" Young Harvey Miller asked his attorney, Fancher Sarchet, this question every time Sarchet visited him in jail. Miller, charged with first-degree murder, awaited trial in Larimer County jail in the summer of 1923.

Sarchet tried to reassure his client: innocent people don't get convicted of crimes they didn't commit, he told the young man. But in his heart, he knew better. He had seen innocents convicted. He was worried.

The facts did not favor Miller. He and the victim, Monty Henderson, had been seen together outdoors shortly before Henderson was shot. An old pistol and a box of shells were found in the basement of the old schoolhouse where Miller, Henderson and their wives were living for the summer. One shell had been exploded. Ballistics tests showed that the spent bullet had come from the pistol found at the scene. The bullet had gone through the victim's eye and lodged in his brain. At the trial, the prosecution brought doctors, the coroner and other witnesses to the stand.

They had means, they had opportunity, but did they have motive? Why would Miller have shot his friend?

Sarchet had developed a theory about the shooting—he believed that it was an accident, that the loaded pistol had been thrown or dropped onto the concrete floor, causing the weapon to discharge and, tragically, go into the fragile area around and in back of the eye. Following a lengthy, exhaustive and, he felt, telling cross-examination of the prosecution's ballistics expert, Sarchet put George Wolfer, who had once seen an accidental shooting that fit Sarchet's theory, on the stand.

Miller then spoke on his own behalf, telling his version of what had occurred: his friend and he had been in the yard chopping wood when

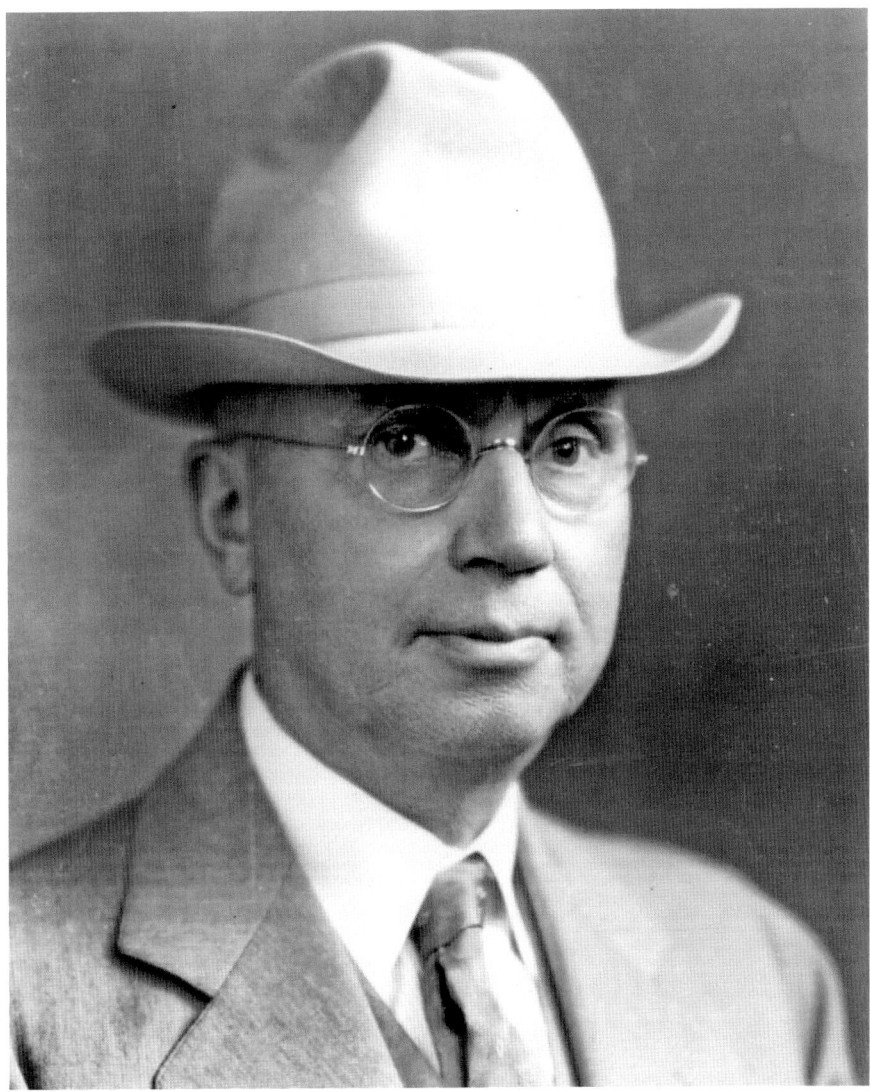

Fancher Sarchet. *LHA H10067.*

Henderson went into the basement. Five minutes later, Miller came in and found him dead. Miller looked, says Sarchet in his book *Murder and Mirth*, pale and tense, his large brown eyes giving him the appearance of "a wounded deer." Sarchet was arguing his case before a jury of strangers, since most of the other candidates had been excused because they knew one or both of the principals in the case.

When it was time for Miller's case to go to a jury of his peers, Miller was taken back to the jail and Sarchet sat down to wait. "These were," he records, "the longest five hours I have ever endured.…Years are short but minutes are long."

At last the jury returned. Miller was brought back in and stood to await his fate. Silence in the room was profound as the verdict was handed from the foreman to the clerk, then to the judge, who then instructed the clerk to read it aloud.

"We the jury…find the defendant, Harvey Miller, not guilty."

Justice had, this time, been served.

The KKK in Colorado

The Ku Klux Klan in Colorado? Hard to believe—the Klan was mainly in the South, wasn't it?

Believe it.

In the aftermath of World War I, the Great War as it was called then, American society adopted a carefree, hedonistic posture, paying little heed to the outside world. America became radically isolationist and patriotic in reaction to the horrendous toll "the war to end all wars" had taken—not only soldiers, but a virulent, cruel flu epidemic following the war that took many lives. The Klan's message of patriotic fervor and nationalism fit right in with the current mood in Colorado and nationwide. Thus, it was not difficult for the KKK to infiltrate the politically dominant Republican Party in Colorado.

This was not the Klan's first foray into our state. History records some isolated incidents in the 1880s, the targets being African Americans, Catholics, Jews and Hispanics. Because few blacks lived in our state at that time, the KKK turned its attention elsewhere and sometimes drove people from their homes. However, it was not until the 1920s that the Klan's actions in Colorado received much attention. The Klan became officially incorporated as an organization in the state, with a goal of "purifying" the state by occupying the majority of public offices, local and statewide. By the mid-1920s, Klan members had successfully elected a governor, lieutenant governor, secretary of state and mayor of Denver. Before long, membership throughout the state was more than thirty thousand.

As it did in other Colorado communities, the Klan arrived in Fort Collins and was accepted as a legitimate organization. Drawn in by the patriotic rhetoric, Samuel Salyers, who owned a small grocery store, joined and was elected exalted cyclops of the Fort Collins klavern in 1924.

Soon afterward, white-robed, hooded Klansmen marched in the streets of our town and rallied on a hill near the town. Salyers finally discovered the depths of the Klan's profound hatred of Catholics and Jews. Deeply dismayed, feeling deceived, Salyers denounced the klavern's prejudicial beliefs. A Christian, he said they should have charity toward all.

The klavern summarily dismissed Salyers. Members of the klavern were told to boycott his grocery store; others would not shop there for fear of retaliation even though they did not belong to the Klan. Salyers faced ruin, but he stood his ground.

We do not know what happened to him subsequently; his grocery store disappears from the city directory a few years after this dramatic confrontation. However, his story received attention throughout Colorado. Not long after what happened here, a statewide bipartisan group began investigating the Klan, ultimately forcing it out of the Republican Party. By 1926, its influence had diminished considerably.

It cannot be said that the Klan completely left Colorado after that; incidents did occur from time to time. But the tide had turned, people were wiser and the KKK never again held such sway. In the years to come, hooded marchers, torches held high, would no longer be seen striding through the city's streets.

Murder on a Winter's Night

On a crisp winter night in February 1934, Viola and Clifford Smith left their small farmhouse near Wellington to attend a 4-H entertainment program at the high school. Their boarder, sixteen-year-old Bobby Griffin, was not feeling well, so they left him at home, sleeping.

The young couple returned home later that evening to find intruders inside: two brothers, Louis and John Pacheco. Bobby lay on the floor, dead. The brothers were demanding wages from Smith, who had hired them to thin sugar beets and withheld their pay because they stole and butchered one of the couple's calves. Words were exchanged; then Louis fatally shot Clifford. Viola was also struck. She fell to the floor. John poured kerosene over the bodies, thinking her dead as well, and callously threw a lit match onto them, lighting the kerosene to destroy the evidence.

Viola, who was only twenty-two, lay absolutely still until the two left. Then she struggled up and managed to beat out the slowly spreading flames. Though seriously wounded, she summoned her courage and went for help. Along the way, she encountered barbed-wire fencing that threatened to snag her; stumbling in the dark, she sometimes had to feel her way along. By sheer dint of will, she made it to the home of her neighbor, Ernest Warner.

Like many rural residents in the depths of the Depression, Warner had no telephone and no car, so he ran a mile to another neighbor, Floyd Jones, who did have a car. They raced for aid—the two criminals were on the loose, and who knew what they might do next? They had already killed two people. Stopping at the first home with a phone, Warner and Jones called a doctor and the sheriff's office. While the doctor arranged to get Viola to the hospital, law officers rushed to the scene.

Sheriff George Saunders, Deputy Frank Ghent and another deputy found no trace of the two murderers in the house. It turned out later that when the murderers saw that one victim had escaped, they went into hiding.

Searching in the dark and stubbled fields was very difficult. There was little to go on; the crime scene had revealed only one .22-caliber bullet. They did not find the fugitives, but when daylight came, someone discovered a human tooth adhering to another bullet. The evidence suggested that the bullet had passed clear through Clifford Smith's head and hit one of the killers in the cheek, loosening the tooth.

That proved to be the case. When the brothers were found soon afterward, hiding in a friend's back bedroom, John Pacheco had a hole in his cheek and a missing tooth. Louis casually admitted to the killings. A swift trial in March, with Viola as a witness, found them guilty and condemned them to die.

Civil Unrest

In the early 1960s, the entire country was restless, anxious and embroiled in racial controversies that seemed, too often, to lead to violence and destruction. In Fort Collins, however, students at the university had, according to author James Hansen, chosen for the most part not to engage in the unrest. A sympathy boycott against the local Woolworth's fell flat.

Following the furor created by James Meredith's attempt to enroll at the University of Mississippi, a 1962 *Collegian* editorial criticized the policy of imposing integration on schools, enforced by the federal government. Letters to the editor on both sides of the issue, mostly from faculty members, failed to ignite interest among the student body.

Then Charles Fager, a member of Farmhouse fraternity, learned that Meredith would be in Denver to give a speech. Boldly, Fager and *Collegian* editor Dennis Lone sent a telegram to Meredith inquiring whether he would be willing to come here and, if so, at what cost.

Meredith responded that he could come for $500 and expenses. Where, the two students wondered, would they get $500? Though neither "was especially popular with the members of this body," they approached the student legislature and won approval for the sum after a difficult negotiation. Meredith, the legislators realized, was sure to be a big draw.

But Fager and Lone still needed money for Meredith's expenses. Fager decided to invite Meredith to stay at his fraternity house, a privilege he enjoyed as a member. However, when he brought the matter before his fraternity brothers, to his surprise and dismay those "mild-mannered brothers of mine" voted to deny the famous black figure their hospitality, saying "the most incredible things. I could not believe my ears." Word of that decision got around the campus quite quickly, "with highly embarrassing ramifications for the Farmhouse fraternity," Hansen notes, and the very next day, the members changed their minds. Meredith could stay with them.

So James Meredith came to Fort Collins to speak in 1963. His appearance was an outstanding triumph—over 1,500 people attended, at fifty cents admission per person, resulting in a profit for the program. In a low-key manner, Meredith spoke about his desire to attend the University of Mississippi as being his father's dream: his father had worked long and hard so his children could have a better life than his. Meredith said he endured "the horrors of Oxford" in order that his father's dream would matter.

The stunning success of Meredith's appearance here led to invitations to other speakers during the 1963–64 academic year, among them Dick Gregory and Mississippi governor Ross Barnett. All the speakers helped to bring the issue of race relations to the forefront, for the university and for the community at large, thanks to two students who decided to do something daring.

Chapter 5
FRONTIER EDUCATION

Citizens of the small town on the river knew how important education was to the town's future. Establishing a school system was a high priority for those who governed. The first school, though, was a private one—Auntie Elizabeth Stone's widowed niece, Elizabeth Keays, arrived in 1866 with her small son, Will. Seeing that the scattered settlement lacked a school, she started teaching her son at home in her aunt's house. Before long, a few other children joined the lessons, and the first school here was in place.

When the town was official a few years later, the founders established a kindergarten in a small building on Riverside Drive, starting the school system that now includes four high schools, numerous middle and elementary schools and thousands of students.

By 1879, the agricultural college had opened its doors to the first class of five students, two of them women. As a land grant college, it was open to both genders even though the majority of colleges and universities nationwide did not yet admit women.

Frontier teachers were nearly all young, single women, though a few men undertook the job. In rural schools, the teacher boarded with the family of a board member, ensuring her acceptable behavior. Standards for behavior were strict—dress must be modest, she must not ever be alone with an unmarried man and she should be seen attending church regularly. Quite often, when a young woman ventured west to become a teacher, she met a suitable young man and married, putting an end to her teaching career. Thus, when Elizabeth Keays married Harris Stratton, a professor at the college, she quit teaching.

The stories in this chapter take us back to a time when education was regimented, focusing on basic subject areas with much memorization; students were expected to behave in prescribed fashions, and classrooms were not, for the most part, scenes of creative learning and thinking. At the university level, the course of study for women was limited to the domestic arts, although they could take classes in other subjects. In the early years, sports had yet to become dominant and popular, though sporting events did take place. Since high school was not commonly part of educational expectations—most students completed eighth grade and stopped—universities in the beginning provided considerable high school–level material.

Like so many other facets of life in our town, education evolved with growth and change. Today's classrooms are vastly different from the ones our forebears knew.

The Coming of the College

All the settlers in the small town that remained after the fort had closed were uncertain about the future. How could the town survive without some incentives? What was needed, they felt, were a railroad through town and a college. The federal Morrill Act of 1862 had established the concept of land grant colleges. Fort Collins wanted one. While others worked on bringing the railroad, Harris Stratton vigorously advanced the idea of securing the college.

State Representative Matthew Taylor introduced a bill to the territorial legislature that would locate the college in Fort Collins. Political machinations of the highest order were required, but the bill was signed into law in February 1870. Now to progress from paper and promises to brick and mortar.

Despite the grasshopper invasion and a severe drought, some determined men took action. In 1873, the local Grange held a picnic on the college grounds (much of which had been donated by local residents) to establish ownership by plowing and seeding twenty acres. It worked—the next year, a small brick building, sixteen by twenty-four feet, was erected on the grounds. The Claim Building, as it was called, was intended for storage of wheat and farm tools, but a few years later, it

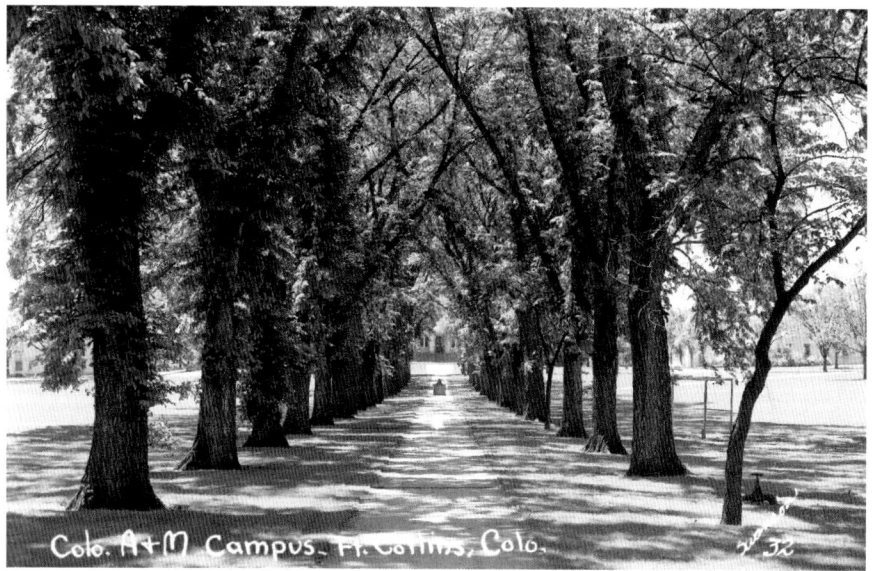

The oval, original center of the college campus. *MEM*.

briefly housed the college's first president, Elijah Edwards (probably not too comfortably).

Statehood in 1876 brought about change—a State Board of Agriculture was established to govern the school, which was to be, as Stratton said, for "the sons *and daughters* of the farmers of Colorado to have an opportunity to attend a college."

With the coming of the railroad in 1877, the survival of the college was assured. That same year, a sturdy, solid structure labeled the Main Building (made with bricks from Auntie Stone's brickyard) graced the campus. It was to stand for almost a century. It began to appear that the college could actually happen.

And happen it did. On the first day of September in 1879, the president and his two faculty members, Ainsworth Blount and Frank Annis, welcomed five students (two of whom were relatives of the president)—two women and three men. By the end of the first term, there were twenty students to study arithmetic, English, history, philosophy, horticulture and farm economy.

Students were required to work at various manual jobs for five or ten cents an hour and to attend chapel services every morning. With the lack of preparatory high schools in the state, a concept not widely in use at the time, students as young as sixteen were then learning what future students would learn in high school.

Today, amid the bustling campus of Colorado State University, it's hard to envision a student body of twenty studying in a single building surrounded by farms and orchards on the outskirts of town. Yet from those small seeds came a mighty university.

Teaching School

Students starting a new school year, teachers readying their classrooms and parents seeing the end of summer invite comparisons with days long past, when teaching school was vastly different than it is today.

Fort Collins held the first kindergarten class west of the Mississippi River. That happened in 1880 thanks to the efforts of Judge Jay Boughton. At first, classes were held in a small building; in 1886, when Remington School was built, the kindergarten moved to the new school. Merle Bennett, who taught kindergarten there for many years starting in 1918, was beloved by her students. She never raised her voice but calmed anxious children with kindness and respect. This writer was privileged to have been taught kindergarten, at the time half-day sessions, by Miss Bennett.

An early twentieth-century teacher, Laura Makepeace, who went on to become a librarian at the college, began teaching in 1911 in a one-room school near Redfeather. The school sessions were seven months long at a salary of fifty dollars a month. To teach, one had only to be eighteen years old and a high school graduate. Certification was required, but the length of the certification depended on the grade received on an examination—70–79 was good for six months, 80–89 for eighteen months and 90 or above for three years. Makepeace, like other rural teachers, lived in a private home, paying about twelve dollars a month for room and board.

When a mother visited the school and offered to provide a stove and cooking utensils if the teacher would prepare a hot meal for the children, Makepeace called other mothers together and arranged for their children to contribute food. She made soup, dumplings and hash, among other hot dishes, and considered these meals the first hot lunches served in Larimer County in a rural school.

Times were different indeed.

The College Dairy Farm

The milk arrived with regularity on the author's front doorstep of her childhood home, contained in gleaming glass bottles inside a small box. Rich and fresh, the milk provided by the college dairy farm was prized for its taste and quality. Her mother skimmed the cream off the top and set it aside in the refrigerator; on Sunday nights, the whole family took turns cranking the ice cream machine to turn it into homemade ambrosia. Nothing equals the taste of ice cream churned at home by hand.

As part of its mission of agricultural research and education, the college started a dairy herd in 1883 with the arrival of a purebred Jersey cow and her calf. Soon the herd, located where the Animal Sciences Building now stands, was producing a bountiful supply of milk. The domestic sciences curriculum of the 1890s included a course in how to make butter. The cows obligingly supplied the ingredients.

According to Gordon "Hap" Hazard, president of the Fort Collins Historical Society, the herd remained on campus until 1954, moving in 1928 to the site where the Military Science Annex was later built. The town was still small enough, the economy still agrarian enough, that no one minded the presence of the cows.

In 1954, the State Board of Agriculture arranged for the purchase of farms owned by the Bay and Hahn families. The farms composed half the land bordered by South College Avenue, West Drake Road, South Shields Street and West Prospect Road. A new dairy farm was constructed there.

But the town continued to grow, pushing west and south. The city annexed the land in 1963, and soon the dairy was surrounded by houses whose occupants did not like the noise and smells emanating from the farm, most noticeable after a rainstorm. Accordingly, the college decided to relocate once again, building a state-of-the-art facility adjacent to the new veterinary college buildings, which had been completed in 1979. In 1981, the herd of 140 cows moved into its new home.

The focus of the university had changed over the years. By the 1980s, the agricultural aspect of its educational mission had become much less prominent. Once again, housing surrounded the new dairy, and in 1989, the State Board of Agriculture decided to end dairy operations and auction off the herd.

Yet the herd left us a memorable legacy: Mama Cow, who achieved a world record of 334,000 gallons of milk over her sixteen years of production. When she died in 1967, she was buried on the site of the dairy.

Outside the Livestock Pavilion on the campus stands a monument to this prolific cow and to a simpler time, long past.

Diversity in Education

For as long as anyone could remember, higher education was the province of the elite—namely, rich young men. Admission was denied to women, minorities and people of lesser means. The place of women was in the home, and the place of workers was in the fields or in the underbelly of a city, certainly not at a well-endowed college that chose applicants with great care.

But then along came the Morrill Act, establishing land grant colleges, in 1862. The intent was to open education to everyone who wished to attend. (Well, almost everyone; minorities were still largely excluded.)

Until the Morrill Act, women who sought a college education had met almost universally with closed doors, but the Agricultural College of Colorado opened its doors to both men and women when classes began in 1879. The students came—from farms, from shops, from homes; one woman was in the first graduating class at the new agricultural college, and more enrolled. The curriculum for women was somewhat different from that for men, more focused on the domestic arts, but thanks to land grant colleges, women could be admitted without having to do battle to get there, with the exception of the School of Veterinary Medicine, which admitted only one woman until the 1960s. Women were able to partake fully of the college experience here from the beginning.

The move to allow admission to minorities resulted in an amended Morrill Act in 1890. It would take time for a significant percentage of minorities to enroll, but in 1891, the first African American came to Fort Collins to go to college. His name was Grafton St. Clair Norman, and he came from Hamilton, Ohio, the same hometown as the college president, Barton Aylesworth. Fort Collins Historical Society president Gordon Hazard speculates that the two may have known each other, which might explain why Norman chose a school so far from home. Norman distinguished himself at the college. As a junior, he won an oratorical competition, and as a senior, he represented the school at a national meeting of the YMCA. He graduated with a bachelor of science degree.

He went on to serve as an engineer in the army during the Spanish-American War, which started in 1898. He helped with the 1900 census. Back in the Midwest, he was a teacher and then an insurance agent. According to Hazard, he also served in the First World War.

It would take a few more decades for Hispanics to join the roll of graduates at the college. Jovita Lobato was the first Hispanic graduate, earning her degree in 1936. She became a teacher and had a long, successful career in education.

The diversity that exists in colleges and universities today came about because of groundbreakers like these who paved the way.

In the Beginning: Campus Life and Sports

In the early days, the oval was ringed with academic buildings, including the library, where students in this photograph, men and women, quietly bend to their books, circa 1910. The Morgan Library, west of the oval, replaced the original building in the 1960s; buildings on the oval took on other uses.

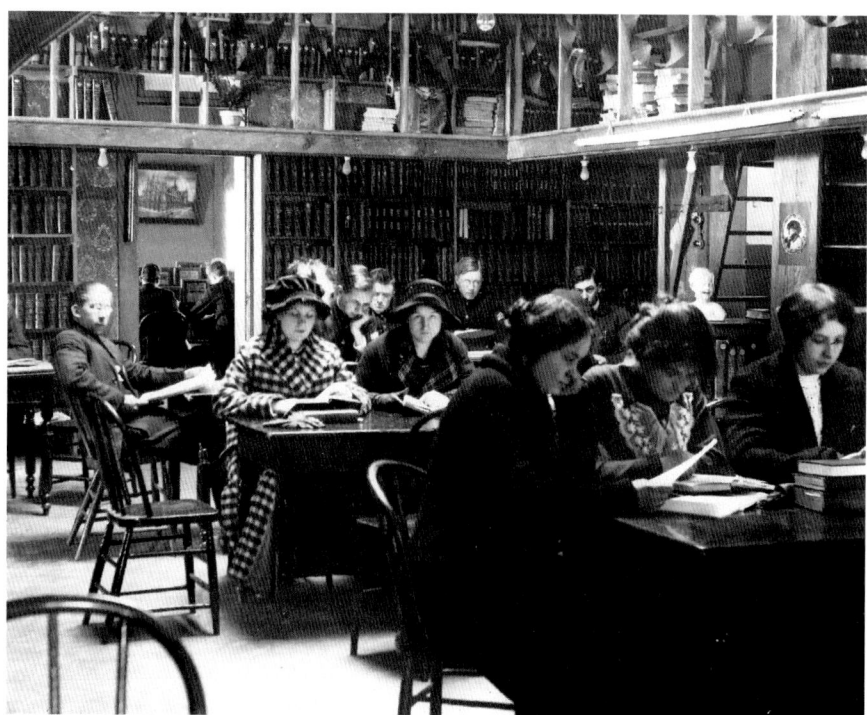

Interior of the first college library. *MEM.*

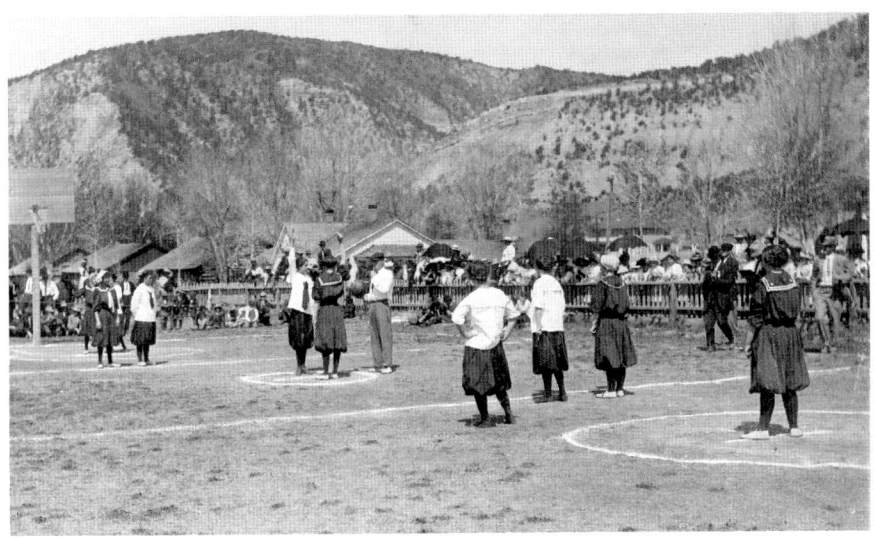

Women playing basketball, circa 1920s. *MEM.*

Women started playing basketball at the college in the 1890s (about the same time that football became official) even though it was not sanctioned by the administration. Despite their lack of status, the teams aroused interest among the student body, working around the lack of a coach, sufficient equipment and a place to play.

Greeks Come to the Campus

Should Colorado Agricultural College (CAC), "democracy's college," as author James Hansen describes it, an institution open to all who wished to enter, allow fraternities and sororities, whose membership was selective and considered elitist, as a presence in college life?

Such a debate arose in 1908, when Greek organizations were beginning to get established on campuses nationwide. On the one hand, the college had no on-campus housing and no dining facilities, the only dormitory having been demolished in 1893. Fraternities and sororities housed and fed their members. Also, with no shared living space and no student center, students had few opportunities to develop friendships outside of academia; Greek houses would offer environments conducive to fellowship.

The organizations, advocates claimed, brought order to student life, promoted responsibility and engendered school spirit. During the early twentieth century, athletics, particularly football, became increasingly important at CAC and other colleges, so this was considered an important factor. Charles Lory, who became college president in 1909, had himself belonged to a fraternity and seemed amenable to the Greeks' presence at the college.

On the other hand, opponents pointed out, these organizations were exclusive: not everyone could afford to join, and not every student was invited. This left out a growing number of students as enrollment increased. And there were always fewer Greek houses, it was noted, than students needing housing.

The debate went on for some years, during which time a couple of local fraternities were formed, but by 1915, the first nationally affiliated fraternities arrived—Sigma Nu and Sigma Phi Epsilon. The national sorority Gamma Phi Beta absorbed local Tau Kappa Sigma.

Greek houses provided a significant portion of student life during this time. By 1925, there were fifteen at the college, hosting dinners and other events. In 1926, according to Hansen, 480 of 1,190 students belonged to a fraternity or sorority. Even in the Depression, these organizations managed to hang on and dominate campus politics as they long had done.

However, Lewis Walt, who was not a member of a fraternity, decided to run for student president during the mid-1930s—and won. One outcome of this was formation of a formal student association. (Walt, a natural leader, went on to become a much-decorated soldier, serving in three wars and rising to the rank of general.)

Another consequence of this political shift was construction of a student center in the late 1930s. The Johnson Student Center on the oval (now the administration building) served both students and faculty until the Lory Student Center was built several decades later. Around this time, too, student housing was constructed on campus, providing an alternative to Greek houses or boardinghouses in town.

From then on, while Greek organizations remained an active part of campus life, they took on a somewhat different role than they had previously played.

High-Altitude Cooking

What a surprise pioneer women must have had when they first baked cakes at five thousand feet! Cake recipes that worked perfectly well at sea level came out of the oven here flat as a pancake or sunken in the middle. Biscuits, light and fluffy at home, were hard as rocks. Yeast bread behaved oddly. Water boiled at a lower temperature, so boiled food took longer to cook. Nothing worked the way a cook might expect it to. No cookbooks existed to help with adjustments; the only thing cooks could do was experiment until they got it right.

No doubt they shared their successes and failures with others and, in time, came to understand how to adjust recipes and to cultivate patience when boiling water to cook vegetables, eggs or anything else. But it must have been a struggle, one seldom noted in all the volumes that have been put to paper about pioneers' experiences on the high plains.

Help was on the way, but it did not come until the new century.

In 1908, Inga Allison joined the home economics faculty at the agricultural college and a few years later headed the department. Schooled at the University of Chicago, she possessed the scientist's innate instincts for research and experimentation.

In his book *Democracy's College in the Centennial State*, James Hansen describes Allison's efforts to uncover the secrets of successful cooking at high altitudes. The department had no laboratory, so all was done with makeshift equipment. With the help of future college president Charles Lory, who was then an instructor of physics, she created a device that could help her determine relative air pressures. An air pump sat atop a jar that sat atop an electric hot plate. A manometer measured air pressure. Thus, she could experiment with various levels of air pressure for cooking food in water.

However, baking was another matter. She and her assistants were gradually able to adjust recipes for this altitude, but for altitudes higher than here, she would have to go up, which is what she did.

Before Trail Ridge Road was built, Fall River Road—a narrow, twisting gravel incline—went over the Continental Divide. At almost twelve thousand feet there was a shelter house, which is where they did their baking experiments, producing "popovers that would not pop and angel food cakes that clung soggily to the bottoms of their pans," says Hansen. Clearly, more research was needed, but it would have to wait until a proper laboratory could be built.

That happened in 1927. The college's high-altitude laboratory, now part of the university extension service, became a primary source for cookbook authors and manufacturers who produced baking mixes for sale. Finally, cooks could make cakes that didn't fall, eggs boiled to perfection and biscuits that didn't bounce.

Painting the Aggie "A"

Before A&M College became Colorado State University, teams were known as Aggies, a term also used to identify students. For as long as most longtimers can remember, a prominent hill west of town has been decorated with a large white "A," a symbol easily taken for granted as simply part of the landscape. It is, but there is a story behind those painted rocks.

In the aftermath of World War I, patriotism and pride in one's institution were prominent in the culture. Universities and colleges began creating large insignias on hillsides to let the world know that they were there. In the early 1920s, students decided to do the same thing here. At a student body assembly on December 4, 1923, the vote was strongly in favor of creating a college emblem—an "A" for Aggies.

Before anything could be done, permission had to be obtained from the landowner, R.G. Maxwell. He agreed to lease the land for one hundred years at one dollar a year. With this matter resolved, work began on December 12, declared a college holiday.

Supervision was delegated to the A Club, a select group of students who had won athletic letters (established in 1913 along with a growing interest in football). The military department agreed to provide transportation, and female students brought food for the workers.

It was no easy task. Working uphill, the students first had to remove brush and move large rocks to form the "A." Since it was December, the weather was brisk. Forming the letter took a full day, so the whitewashing was postponed for a week. That required getting whitewash up the hill bucket by bucket. Each bucket of whitewash went through many hands before it was applied. *Democracy's College in the Centennial State* contains a photograph that shows the buckets winding their way uphill.

The volunteers who bent their backs that day had not exactly volunteered—they were freshmen, and roll call was taken before the project began. Anyone who failed to show up was under pressure of criticism for his absence. (Some professors also took part, one supposes willingly.)

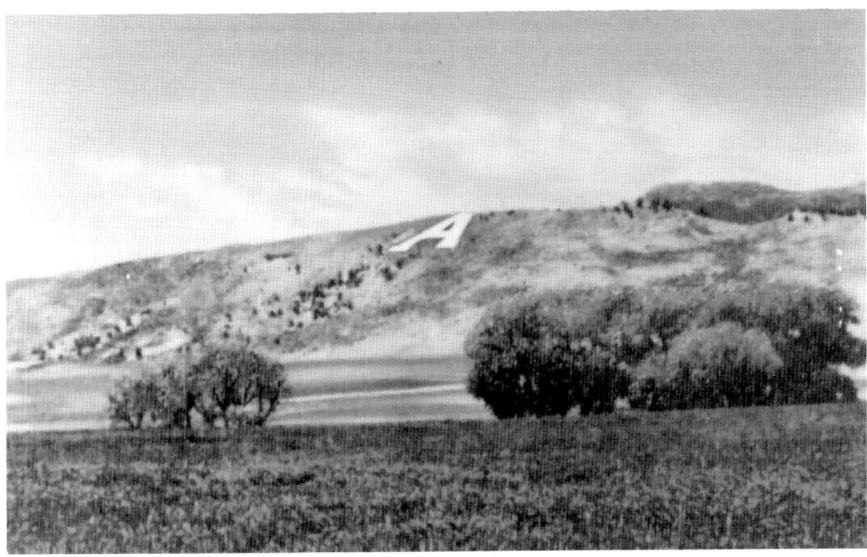

The Aggie "A." *LHA H09077.*

A few years later, some remodeling was done to make the legs longer and lower the bar across the center. The result was legs 450 feet long with a 250-foot width across the bottom. Each leg of the letter was 40 feet wide. The size has not been changed again. Refreshing the "A" became an annual ritual, part of the college's traditions.

Today, CSU teams are Rams, and the university's emphasis is far wider than agriculture. The "A" is no longer whitewashed but coated with an environmentally friendly paint. Student volunteers do the job under the auspices of the Alumni Association before the first home football game. Thanks to them, the "A" endures.

Through a Student's Eyes

The high-ceilinged room, hot in fall and spring and cold in winter, held rows of wooden desks, each with its inkwell under the lift-up cover, each lid scarred with carvings. Underneath were stored pencils, crayons, erasers, school books and paper.

Tall, narrow, smudged windows let in filtered sunlight. A naked bulb hung from the ceiling in the center of the room. At the front of the room stood the teacher, a formidable woman with hair sternly secured in a bun, eyes that seemed to see everyone and everything at once and sturdy shoes that would get her through the long day. She wore a solid-color dress that hung almost to her ankles, belted loosely at the waist.

An air of respect—perhaps lightly tinged with fear—pervaded the classroom. When the teacher rapped her ruler on the desk for silence, the room was entirely still. When she called on a student, he or she promptly stood to answer the question or recite or to go to the blackboard. When a student misbehaved, as some did from time to time, the miscreant was sent to the principal's office to receive a smack or two from the paddle that hung on the wall there—an accepted consequence seven or eight decades ago.

Recess was a joyous time, a time of letting go. Girls in their blouses, cardigans and knee-length skirts and boys in their neatly pressed shirts and trousers swung from the monkey bars, one arm at a time, or climbed to the top of the slide and flew down again and again. They moved their legs energetically to pump the swings, going as high as they dared. Occasionally a student would land hard on the gravel playground, scraping a knee or an elbow, but the unfortunate child would waste no precious recess time on tears. In a separate area, the younger students played in the sandbox or on the low swings. Older boys might move to the sidewalk to wield marbles with their expert thumbs; older girls might be nearby playing jacks or hopscotch.

Students brought brown-bag lunches. For a nickel, they could buy a small carton of milk to accompany their sandwiches.

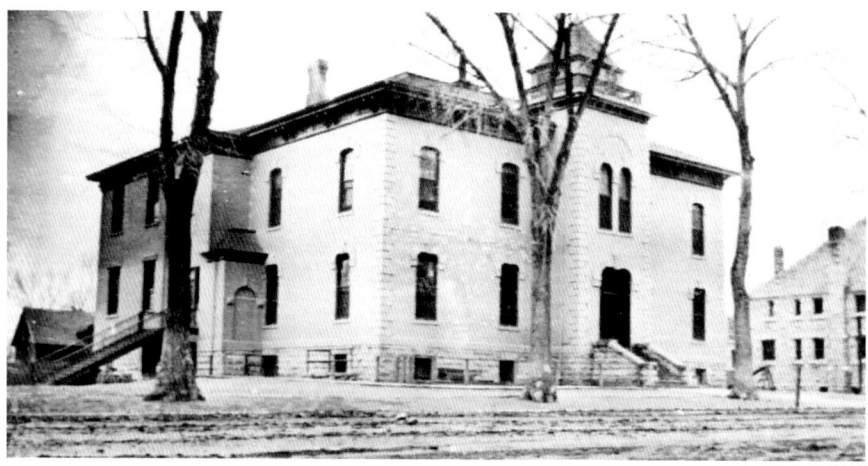

Remington School was named for Colonel John Remington, an early investor in the town. *LHA H05501.*

Even though this would appear to be a hostile place, one that students might enter with fear and trembling, that was by no means the whole story at Remington School, that long-gone, sturdy stone structure on Remington Street. Inside those rather inhospitable classrooms, considerable learning took place. The teachers (for several of whom schools have subsequently been named) possessed a remarkable range of knowledge about many different subjects. They encouraged the students to puzzle out mysteries for themselves and to dive into the unknown with zeal and curiosity. Students may first have entered the building with trepidation, but they departed with a solid foundation for their future educations.

Eddie Hanna

He was lithe and quick on the football field. He was, like so many other veterans right after World War II, going to college on the GI Bill, with plans for his future. He was also on the cusp of integration of sports in America, a black man playing what had long been exclusively a white man's game—slowly changing the culture.

Eddie Hanna, who served in the U.S. Air Force during the war, came to Colorado A&M College in 1947. Weighing not quite 165 pounds, he helped score a touchdown in the Aggies' first game of the season that year against the Colorado School of Mines. He had only entered the game in the fourth quarter but racked up fifty-one yards in that short time. He was instrumental in subsequent victories that season, and in 1948, he led the team to its first-ever bowl game, the Raisin Bowl. Although the Aggies lost to Occidental College in Fresno, California, in a tight contest, Hanna ran seventy-nine yards for a touchdown.

His friendly, easygoing manner contributed to team spirit. Popular with the fans, he was equally well regarded by his teammates, and he held his own academically.

Early in the 1949 season, his last with the school, the Aggies played against Colorado College in Colorado Springs. Although Hanna had mentioned to Coach Bob Davis the day before that he was feeling a little under the weather, he played that day. With the game tied at seven to seven in the fourth quarter, he sprinted to the goal line for a touchdown. Once again, Hanna had saved the day.

The team headed home on the chartered train, triumphantly celebrating. But they had not gone far when Hanna complained of a burning sensation in his chest. Shortly afterward he collapsed; then he died. The date was September 17, 1949. He was twenty-four years old.

The cause of death was discovered to be cardiac arrest. Unknown to his doctors, Hanna had a defective heart. At that time, cardiac care was far from the sophisticated diagnosis and treatment options available today. It is probable that, even had physicians known of his medical condition, they would not have been able to develop a successful treatment program, with so much information about heart disease waiting to be revealed. Like treatments for heart disease, full integration of American athletics came after Hanna's death.

The university has honored him—a scholarship in his name is open to students in the Health and Human Sciences Department. Even though many decades have passed since young Eddie Hanna's life came to a tragic end, he is remembered in the CSU Athletic Department. Two numbers in CSU's football program have been retired: number 48, that of Thurman "Fum" McGraw, for whom the university's athletic center is named, and Eddie Hanna, number 21.

Fort Collins High School

The culture then was in sharp contrast to the twenty-first century.

Students at Fort Collins High School in the early 1950s adhered to a dress code—girls wore calf-length dresses or skirts with decorous blouses; boys wore slacks and buttoned shirts. Bearing books in their arms, the students moved from class to class in an orderly fashion. Couples could do no more than hold hands—to be caught kissing meant a visit to the girls' advisor's office (for the girl) and a scolding (for the boy). Even during lunch time, students could not leave the grounds except to go across the street to the park. Lunch was whatever the cafeteria had on the menu that day.

Unaware of the dangers, knowing only that it made them feel sophisticated, some students smoked—but never on school grounds. That way lay suspension at the very least. Not readily available in Fort Collins at the time, alcohol was not a major form of rebellion for students. Drug use was rare and well concealed. Several boys had cars—if they could afford them, souped-up muscle cars—and drove them proudly to school; most students walked, biked or rode the bus. The car owners delighted in dragracing along College Avenue on Saturday night, risking a ticket.

When a couple was "going steady," the girl wore her boyfriend's class ring on her finger. If the couple broke up, everyone in school knew about it. Not infrequently, couples who dated in high school married after graduation.

Despite outward appearances, no one could have called this an idyllic, naïve or placid time. A generally unacknowledged tension rippled throughout the school, the city—indeed, the whole country—due to the frigidity of the Cold War and the advent of nuclear weapons and, for the boys, the Korean conflict and the draft that awaited them. Yet hedonism was not the reaction; the cultural undercurrents of the time dictated behaviors and choices. Respect for and acceptance of authority prevailed. Teachers always dressed formally and were addressed by their courtesy titles; disrespect was dealt with swiftly. Much as they might have wanted to, students usually chose not to "go all the way." (Education about natural processes was assumed to take place in the home, although reproduction might be delicately approached in biology class or PE.) Girls expected to marry and raise a family, boys to have careers and support the family. If they did plan to go to college, girls' career choices were limited to traditionally female occupations such as teaching, nursing or office work (or acquiring an MRS degree). Boys played football; girls led cheers. Boys played intramural sports; girls played for fun or exercise.

Thanks to the dedicated teachers who taught and guided them, in that era graduates from the handsome brick school with the tempting tower, wide stairways and enduring traditions came away with a solid education whether their time in high school was happy and memorable or otherwise.

The education and experiences gained there, in that different time, served them well wherever life led them after graduation.

Chapter 6

Memorable Places, Local Landmarks

By what measures do we mark the passing of time? Sometimes, it is by the aging, alteration or disappearance of landmarks—or by their sturdy implacability as time moves around them. One of the latter is Horsetooth Mountain in the foothills west of town, which from a distance does indeed look to be a giant tooth. That distinctive landmark is untouched by time. Its story is told in this chapter.

Beginning as an agricultural center of commerce, Fort Collins has grown and evolved far beyond those early days. Flush with the headiness of growth, especially following the Second World War, residents and those charged with governing saw little reason to preserve old landmarks, some of which were crumbling, beyond repair without great expense. That, however, was not a new phenomenon; as far back as the 1870s, landmarks were disappearing, beginning with the old fort.

The only fort remnant to survive for a time, Old Grout, lost out to progress before the turn of the twentieth century. In 1911, a grand hotel, the Tedmon, was razed along with other structures.

Downtown Fort Collins, which has been preserved more or less as it once was, served as a model for Main Street in Disneyland thanks to Harper Goff, who lived here as a child, and that helped ensure its survival—altered but retaining its bones. Avery House—the home of Franklin Avery, who laid out the town in 1872—has been lovingly preserved. This chapter revisits some former landmarks, long gone, that once had pride of place in our town, a few that are still standing and some memorable sites.

Notable places offer us a window into a past long gone; time and progress bring ineradicable change. This chapter reminds us of what was and what still is.

Legendary Landmarks

From a distance, it's easy to see why the distinctive rock formation atop the highest of the foothills west of town is called Horsetooth. It gives the appearance of a tooth belonging to a (very, very large, perhaps prehistoric) horse. So it would be tempting to conclude that this is the story behind the name. Simply that.

Not quite. Like most stories, the legends of Horsetooth Mountain are more involved. Actually, the source of the name itself is unknown, but there are legends relating to the shape of the rock; therein lie the tales.

In the time before, an Arapaho legend says, the Great Red Warrior and the Great Black Warrior fought a fierce battle. It was a savage contest that went on for a long time. The Great Black Warrior eventually killed the Great Red Warrior, whose blood, falling from the heavens, colors the rock for all eternity. This legend, however, does not account for the large gaps on either side of the "tooth"—though perhaps they were caused by the warriors attacking each other.

Another Native American legend attributes the rock formation to the downfall of a sleeping giant. This giant was evil and would not permit the warriors to hunt in the Valley of Contentment, where deer, buffalo and other game were abundant. (The valley so named now lies under the reservoir and was once the site of a lively town, but that's another story.) This angered their leader, Chief Maunamoku (named Great Buffalo in some accounts), who decided that the time had come to slay the giant. But how to do it? The giant would kill any who tried to hunt in the valley. It was said that the rock at the top of the mountain was his beating heart, and they did not dare venture close. The chief and his warriors conferred. They needed the game to survive.

They knew that a night hawk guarded the giant. If they could distract the bird for a few moments, there might be enough time to slip in for the kill. Hawks are hunters, as were the Native Americans, so they decided to put some prey nearby, which was sure to attract the bird. Quietly, with great stealth and the cover of night, they snared a rabbit to entice the hawk away.

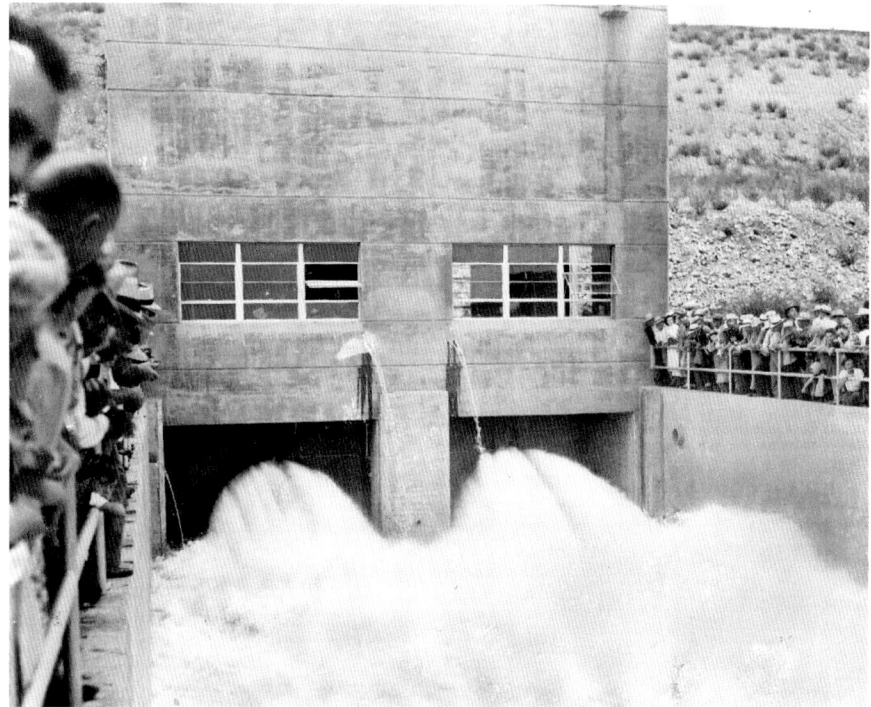

Dedication of Horsetooth Dam. *MEM.*

It worked. Quickly one of the braves, Flying Eagle, scrambled up to the giant's heart, taking his tomahawk. When he got close enough, he reached out and struck with mighty force. But the giant started to rise. With great courage, Flying Eagle slashed again on the other side of the heart, and the giant fell back, dead. The valley was now theirs to hunt in without fear. The gaps between the "tooth" and the rest of the mountain on either side are the slashes Flying Eagle made with his powerful tomahawk. Those who venture to climb the rock (a challenging task) will discover the red color that stains it—which can only be the giant's blood.

Today, Horsetooth Rock tempts climbers and has given its name to the reservoir contained within the foothills formations. In the photograph, on the day of its dedication spectators watch the first release of water upon completion of the Horsetooth Dam project in 1951, construction of which completely submerged the quarry town of Stout, the fertile valley once so coveted by hunters.

Other local rocks have their own stories to tell.

To travelers passing by on U.S. Highway 287 north of Laporte, one ordinary-looking rock, though covered with graffiti, probably does not merit a second glance. But it does have a name and a story. Locals call it Haystack Rock.

The tale, according to author John Hafnor, began during the Civil War. The war had come close to Colorado with the 1862 Battle of Glorieta Pass in New Mexico, a confrontation sometimes compared to Gettysburg as critical to victory for the North. A number of captured Confederate soldiers were assigned to guard the supplies of hay at Camp Collins, feed that was essential for the survival of cavalry soldiers' horses. When a farmer showed up one day in 1863 offering to sell a large supply of hay to the army, the post commander quickly took him up on it, paid him in full after an officer had verified that the stack was indeed there and sent a delegation of soldiers to collect the hay.

When they struck their pitchforks into the stack, the soldiers came upon a surprise. There was hay all right, but underneath it was a large, haystack-shaped rock. The farmer had put one over on the military. Neither history nor Hafnor records what became of the farmer, but it's safe to assume that he never tried that trick on the army again. Perhaps he even used his ill-gotten proceeds to move elsewhere.

Another version comes from David Harris, published in the *Triangle Review* in the 1970s. The boulder, he says, stands out for being the only one of the many Dakota sandstone boulders that broke away from the cliff thousands of years ago to land intact, right in the middle of the valley. Migrants coming along the Overland Trail passed by the rock, which Harris explains is slowly sinking into the valley floor.

This rendition says that it was the Overland Stage Company, operating most actively in the 1860s, that needed to purchase hay for its horses. Coincidentally, the rock was located on ranch land not far from the Laporte Stage Station. Six to eight horses pulled the fast-moving coaches, and the horses, quite naturally, got hungry.

A representative from the stage company approached the rancher to ask if he had any hay to sell. Told that yes, he had some to spare, the buyer named a low price and was surprised when the rancher took him up on it. He paid the rancher before he could change his mind, thinking he had gotten a bargain. Some bargain. Again, just enough hay covered the rock to conceal it, and again the farmer (same one? different one? nobody knows…) got away with it. If it was actually the same farmer and there are two real stories, he was quite the con man. In any event, something of this nature certainly happened.

Another rock with a story to tell is found in Poudre Canyon. Although sometime in the 1880s "Tiger" Jim Wilson is said to have committed a murder on this rock, today Picnic Rock is a favorite stopping place for motorists. Perched on a small sandy cove about ten miles up the canyon, it is a shady, relaxing spot beside the flowing river. The distinctive rock formation once overhung the canyon road but was blasted apart in 1938 for safety reasons, leaving the unusual shape shown here.

All of these unique formations are enduring parts of our local landscape.

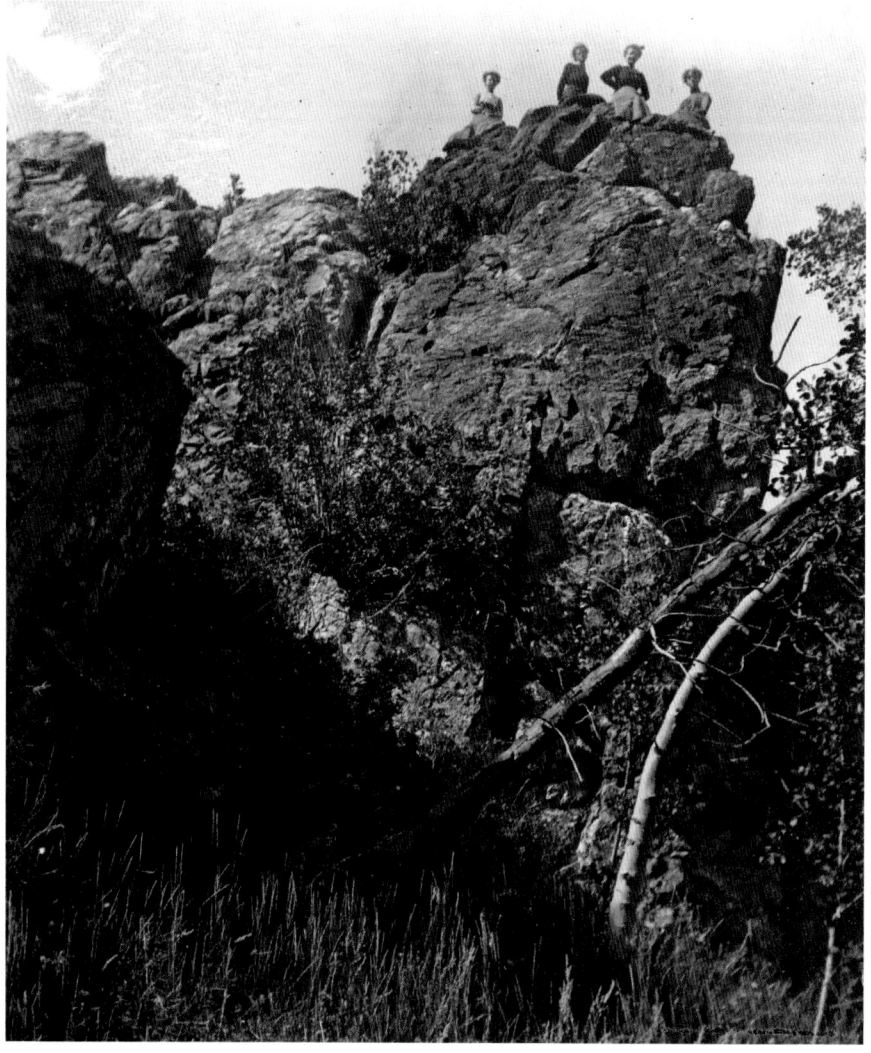

Picnic Rock. *LHA H5971.*

High Up in the Canyon

Many resorts once offered canyon motorists respite as they traveled. In the early days of automobiles, climbing up the canyon could take most of a day, and cars might overheat along the way. Reaching the top, motorists could first stop at Kinikinik Resort for gas, ice and snacks—and probably some water for the radiator—before going on to cross Cameron Pass onto the Western Slope. Long gone now, Kinikinik once had cabins, a store and top-notch fishing.

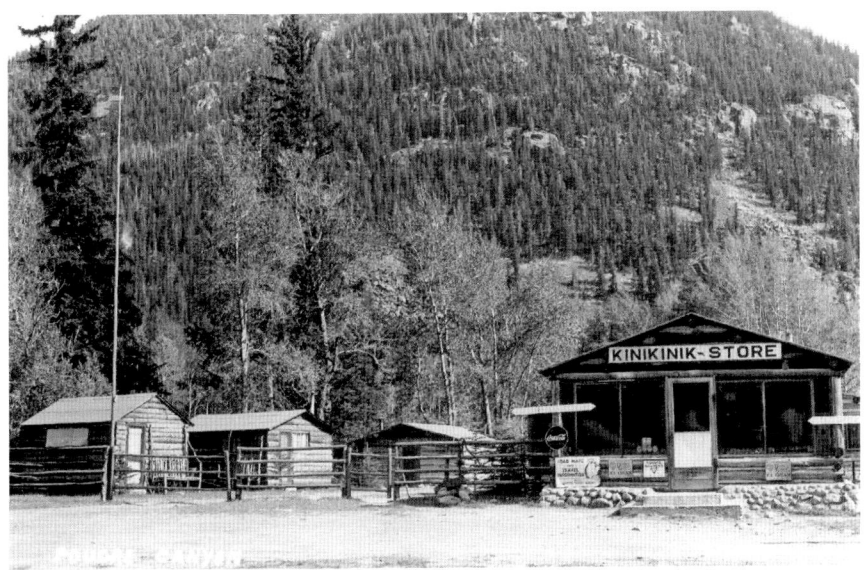

Kinikinik resort. *MEM.*

Old Grout

Old Grout was coming down. Flush with prosperity, giddy with growth, the young town on the Poudre River gave little thought to the past, so when the last vestige of the fort that once stood here was due to be razed, no one seemed concerned.

Ah, but it was Old Grout! What tales that venerable building could have told. Fully revealed, says Ansel Watrous, its history "would read almost like a romance."

Built in 1866 by Joe Mason and Asaph Allen as a sutler's store (in the Old West, a sutler was one who provided supplies shipped from the East) at Jefferson and Linden Streets, the sturdy structure was subsequently owned and operated by John Mathews and Arthur Patterson, then by William Stover; in 1873, it housed a drugstore.

The two-story building had a storeroom, warehouse and living area on the first floor and a public hall, accessed by an outdoor stairway, on the second floor. An expansive front porch and second-floor balcony completed the design.

The only public hall in town, it was used for church services, including a Catholic Mass, dances, theater performances and lectures, along with policy and political debates. For a time, Old Grout became the county courthouse, the great hall serving as the courtroom; another part of the building was used as the jail (from which the infamous outlaw known only as Happy Jack effected a successful escape, never to be seen again). Old Grout, the community gathering place, also housed the local post office at one time.

Curiously, Mason's original partner, Captain Asaph Allen, disappeared in 1869 "as if the earth had opened up and swallowed him," reports Watrous. Allen got off a train in Baltimore as he was heading back to Colorado and was never heard from again. The settlement of his estate, which was sizable, was the first significant case to come before the county court in Old Grout.

In his book *Cache la Poudre*, Herbert Myrick says of Old Grout that it was made of "homely" material, a durable mixture of lime, cement, sand and gravel "also called concrete." He described a dinner given in the hall by Chief Friday that was attended by Utes as well as Friday's Arapahos, an event that ended with some of the women in Friday's tribe leaving him for "the handsome Utes." This colorful story is historically in some doubt, for it has not otherwise been verified, but it may have had a grain of truth—the old building was the scene of many myths and stories.

But public sentiment changes and progress continues apace. Old Grout came down in a cloud of dust and rubble in 1881 to make way for William Stover's new drugstore. "Old Grout, Your Days Are Numbered" trumpeted a newspaper headline—and indeed they were.

A Free Public Library

Once a week, sometimes more often, the author goes to the Old Town Library on Peterson Street. Like most patrons, she does not often stop to think about what it means to have a free public library, accessible to all.

But in the 1800s, most books were held in private libraries by those who could afford them. In some areas, subscription libraries were available for an annual fee, with a limited choice of books (after all, ladies, the majority of readers, could not be exposed to anything offensive). Only those who were able to afford the fee could use them.

As the new century approached, the concept of public libraries supported by taxpayers and free to all took hold. In 1899, the Woman's Christian Temperance Union was instrumental in forming a public library association here. The WCTU collected about eight hundred books, many of them donated by the Reverend George Falconer of Unity Church. At first, the library was housed on the second floor of the Welch Block on College Avenue.

Soon afterward, Mayor Frank Baker appointed a board of directors, and the city took ownership of the public library. The collection grew.

Around 1901, industrial magnate Andrew Carnegie began sharing his wealth for the public good. One of his philanthropies was to endow public libraries. The recipient municipality was required to provide the land and maintain the building and grounds; Carnegie would pay for the building.

A group of dedicated citizens set out to obtain a Carnegie library in Fort Collins. Some sources assert that one of the reasons the ascetic Scotsman approved the petition was that Fort Collins was dry, with many churches. In any event he did approve, financing construction with $12,000. The façade of sandstone came from the quarry at Stout. The building housed almost four thousand volumes when completed in 1904.

The library was to undergo changes, including an addition in the 1930s to create an auditorium. In time, it outgrew the space, and in 1977, a new library opened on the east side of Lincoln Park.

The Carnegie became, for a good many years, the Fort Collins Museum.

Growth inevitably brings change. Today, the Carnegie has experienced another change to become the home of an arts center, and the museum has a new home on Mason Court. But anyone who frequented that old library as a child, as this author did, surely has memories of the high-backed, overstuffed chairs in the reading room, of the ramp that led to the bookshelves in the grown-up library (how exciting it was to be old enough to go up there!), of the sturdy wooden study tables, of the auditorium, scene of many recitals, and of the code of silence: a free public library, open to all.

Once-Thriving Industries

Luther Miller could turn his hand to almost anything, but he made a good living selling his alabaster creations up and down the Front Range. Miller fashioned his pieces with handmade equipment in his house on Whedbee Street and quarried the stone in Owl Canyon. He spent time in a Civilian Conservation Camp in the 1930s to support his family, helping to build Trail Ridge Road, and he worked sugar beet harvests as well. He and his wife, Desdemona, had four sons. Miller was one of several industrious individuals who made a living carving alabaster even during the Depression.

Another successful industry here was Seder Plastics. A two-story, free-standing brick building on North College Avenue serves as a testament

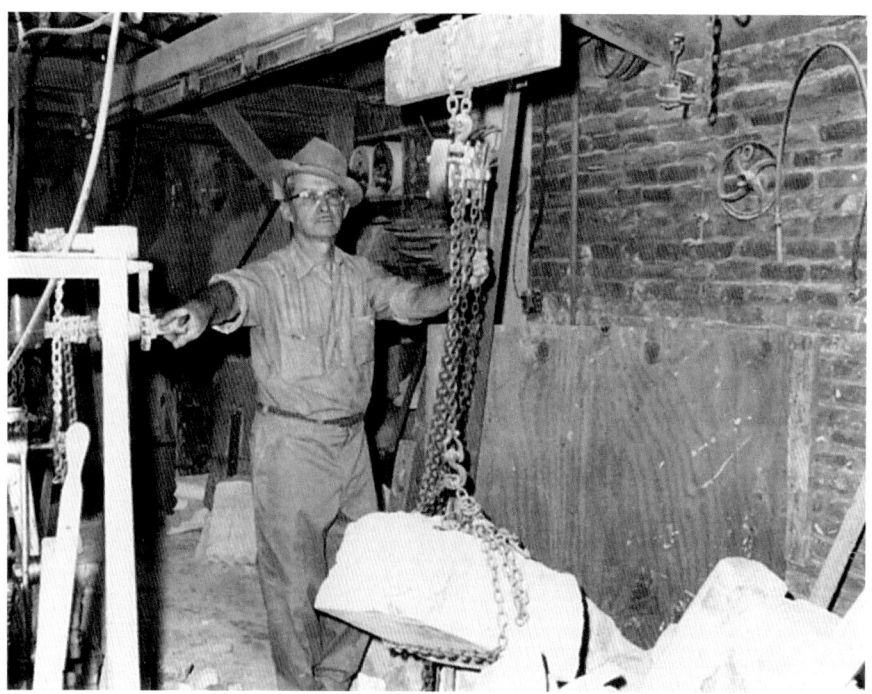

Luther Miller. *Courtesy of Marilyn Miller Van Ausdall.*

to what was, decades ago, a thriving local factory manufacturing plastic products. Quite a few area residents worked at the factory at one time or another. A faded sign at the top of the front façade reads "Molded Products."

The first plastic molding company in Colorado, Ingwersen Manufacturing, was started in Denver in 1928 by G.F. Ingwersen and his brother-in-law, William Colson, a 1913 graduate of Colorado Agricultural College (now Colorado State University) with both civil and electrical engineering degrees. Colson designed presses and dies for molding plastic, and in 1934, his son-in-law, John Gano Seder, used them to start a plastics manufacturing company in Fort Collins, Seder & Son Molded Products Company, providing welcome employment. (The son, John Jr., was born in 1933.)

In 1942, after World War II broke out, Seder purchased the building at 300 North College Avenue for his growing company. Seder Plastics soon became a major employer here and contributed heavily to the war effort by manufacturing essential aircraft components.

The company also made plastic dishware used by airlines, including Continental, to serve passengers meals—now a vintage collectors' item available online. The company's various other products, among them an ashtray designed and patented by Seder (at a time when smoking was widespread), were distributed throughout the United States and in some foreign countries.

Seder Plastics was doing well, labeled by the *Denver Post* as "one of the city's fastest-growing industries," when, in 1951, John Gano Seder Jr. contracted polio, as did several other people in the area. A highly infectious disease that often led communities to declare quarantines and close businesses, poliomyelitis can cause debilitating muscle weakness that strikes particular areas of the body, most frequently the legs. At that time, it tended to especially affect youths. In John Jr.'s case, the disease put him in an iron lung for several years. Sadly, he had contracted polio just a year before Dr. Jonas Salk developed an effective polio vaccine. The younger Seder eventually went to college, but complications from polio set in, and he did not live to take over his father's company. In May 1961, at age fifty-two, John Gano Seder died as well. The company relocated in 1963, leaving the old brick building for others to occupy.

Despite the sadness of losing his only son, the dreamed-for heir to his company, Seder was considered a generous employer and citizen. Like his son, his bookkeeper had been stricken with and crippled by polio.

Today, only the ghost sign remains to recall the heydays of Seder's once-bustling business.

Loved by Locals

Not many people have lived here long enough to remember Toliver's Hardware Store, which began in the 1920s as a gas station and hay merchant and expanded to hardware. In the 1940s, the company was still selling gas, as the photograph shows. After being on the northwest corner of College Avenue and Mason Street for several decades, the store moved around the corner into a Mason Street storefront, discontinuing gasoline sales. Longtimers perhaps recall going into the store, with its creaky floors and knowledgeable clerks who could meet any hardware request, no matter how unusual.

When Julian Siegel came to Fort Collins in the 1920s, he sold hosiery out of a suitcase. He soon expanded to clothing, which was profitable enough to open a women's clothing store on South College Avenue in the 1940s. Ready-to-wear clothing off a rack was not common at the time, especially in Fort Collins, which had catalogue outlets but not a department store, but Siegel made a success of it with his outstanding customer service. The store has since been reopened as a boutique, with the same name and location but a different owner.

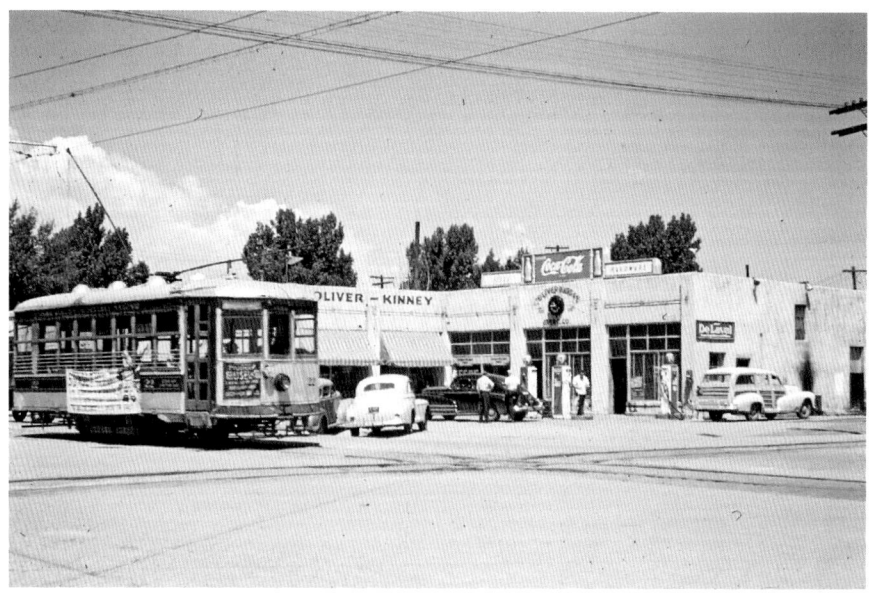

Toliver's hardware store. *MEM*.

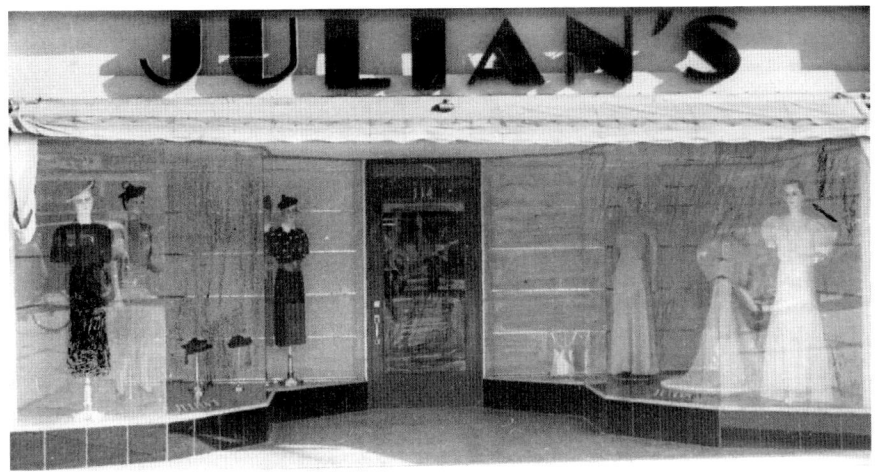

Julian's clothing store. *MEM.*

Agnes Vaille Shelter

Adventurers who tackle the east face of Long's Peak come across the Agnes Vaille Shelter at about thirteen thousand feet. They might well ask, "Who was Agnes Vaille, and why does a shelter bear her name?"

Known among mountaineers as an experienced and fearless climber who had scaled a number of fourteeners, Vaille decided to ascend the east face in the winter. Such a feat had not been accomplished by 1924, when she made her decision to attempt it.

She knew it was unwise to go alone, so she asked her friend and fellow climber Walter Kiener to accompany her. At that time, aids such as sophisticated protective gear and equipment, now *de rigueur* for mountain climbers, were not available. Still, she was determined to make the attempt. Friends described her as always ready for a challenge.

This climb was indeed a challenge. Vaille and Kiener set out on January 11, 1925, with temperatures registering well below zero. They attained the summit the next morning but had not gotten sufficient sleep during the night; both were visibly tired. As they began their descent, Kiener could see how exhausted his friend was. Yet she insisted she was all right, and they kept on.

Then she fell. Sliding down a snowy bank more than 150 feet, she landed in the snow below and, when he reached her, was immobile. A little rest would restore her, she assured him. He could not get her up again. She told him that her hands and feet were partially frozen. He knew he needed to go for help. So he made her as comfortable as possible and set off. The weather was worsening, with a high wind and whipping snow; it took him more than two hours to arrive at Timberline Cabin, where a rescue party was gathering because the two climbers had not returned on time.

Amid a blinding snowstorm, they set out to rescue the stranded hiker. The fierce weather forced two of the rescuers to turn back—one, Hubert Sortland, lost his way and died. Kiener and Jacob Christian finally found her that afternoon. When the rescuers came upon her body, Agnes Vaille lay with her prized axe in her hand, her head pillowed on her knapsack, just as Kiener had left her. In their account of the incident, authors Ben Fogelberg and Steve Grinstead relate that she probably would not have lived long after Kiener left her to go get help.

But the intrepid climber left a legacy, perhaps as an inadvertent reminder that, as Fogelberg and Grinstead comment, the mountain must be respected, ascended and descended with care and humility, at appropriate times of the year, for on what some have called "Colorado's favorite mountain" the forces of nature are extremely powerful.

Looking Back at Downtown

College Avenue, seen in this picture sometime in the 1920s, was the main thoroughfare through town, becoming the road that led to Denver. Most of the original brick structures still stood, though their uses were different from when the town began—restaurants instead of saloons and barbershops, drugstores and office buildings along with hotels.

By the 1930s, movie-going was well established with the American public, especially since the advent of talking pictures. Fort Collins had two theaters, the America and the Lyric. Saturday matinees were popular with school-age children, who paid a dime for a double feature plus cartoons. Both theaters are long gone, but a newer Lyric Theater in a different location still provides entertainment for downtown movie fans.

For more than forty years, the Strang elevator remained downtown, a remnant of times long past. Once upon a time, Fort Collins was a major agrarian center, emerging amid farms and ranches, with services to accommodate the business of agriculture. Once upon a time, a tall grain elevator—for decades the tallest building in town—stood on North Mason Street, a repository for grain to feed sheep and cattle. Flanked by silos, the

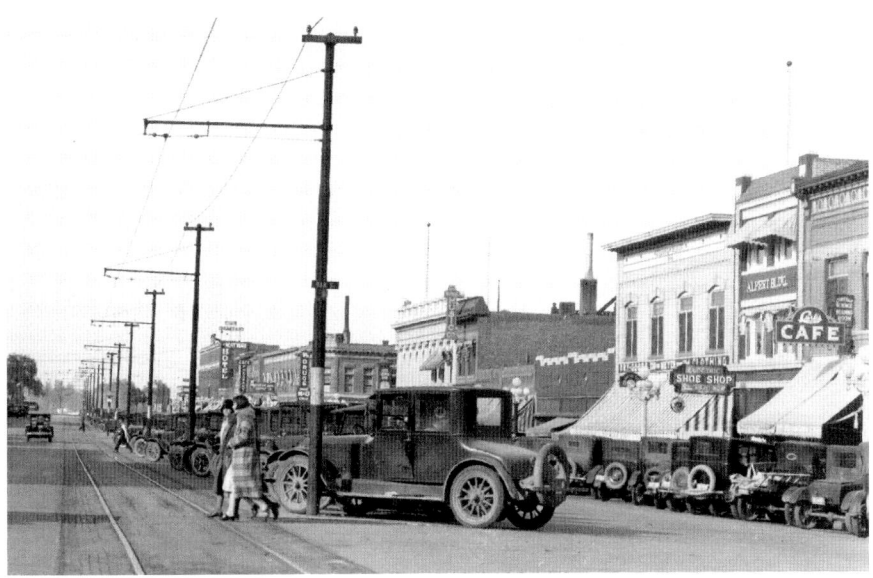

College Avenue, circa 1920s. *MEM.*

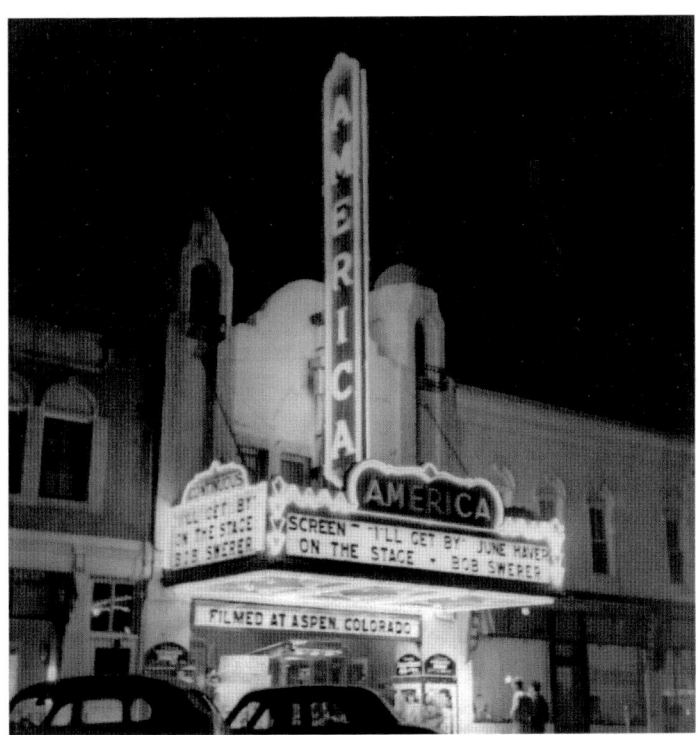

America Theater. *LHA H16765.*

elevator was so essential in the 1920s that the mill operated twenty-four hours a day.

Robert Strang owned and operated the business, which began in 1920 during an era when some spoke of our town as the sheep-feeding capital of the world. The son of Scottish immigrants, Strang paid off the previous owners of the elevator by buying shares as he could afford them. By 1931, while the Great Depression was exerting a stranglehold on the economy, he had a controlling interest, but farmers were struggling to make ends meet. Though known for being frugal, Strang allowed farmers to delay payments on seed until their crops were harvested. Payment for grain was sometimes in produce rather than money. Strang's frugality kept him from replacing the wood stove in his office with electric heat, but he paid his workers in full every Saturday night (while complaining, during the Depression, about two-dollars-an-hour wages).

During World War II, author Arlene Ahlbrandt recalled, an air raid siren sat atop the elevator. Even in the middle of the country, precautions were taken in the event of an air attack.

Strang's father, James Strang, came to Fort Collins in 1888 and settled in Timnath with his wife, Annie Meikle Strang, and his sons. The home he built was situated near the Robert Strauss cabin, and it was to the Strang cabin that the elderly Strauss headed during the devastating flood of 1904. Stranded overnight near a barbed-wire fence, Strauss died the next day of exposure and exhaustion after being carried to his neighbor's home.

Of course, time marches on. In 1969, Robert Strang sold the elevator to Edgar Seaworthy, who used it only to store grain. But Fort Collins was losing its agricultural foundation, growing in population and sophistication and nurturing a broader culture. After forty years, the Strang elevator was no longer the tallest building in town, eclipsed by multi-story buildings rising along College Avenue. The nature of the town had shifted dramatically away from agriculture to commerce and industry. The elevator had outlived its time.

So one day it came down, a last vestige of this town's agricultural origins. Writer Liam Rooney commented that community interest in preserving the elevator was low, being generally reserved for residences and offices—built, ironically, with money made from agriculture. On June 5, 1983, the elevator and silos crumbled into dust, leaving nothing but "fond memories," said Ahlbrandt—memories of a time long past.

Civilian Public Service Camps

They came from all over the country, young men whose consciences and/or religious tenets prevented them from killing other human beings. To satisfy their military obligation, the U.S. government determined that conscientious objectors (COs) could perform "tasks of national importance" on the homefront. Therefore, in 1942, President Franklin Roosevelt issued an executive order creating the Civilian Public Service Program, placing it under the aegis of Selective Service. About twelve thousand men, along with a few women, joined the program. The men were sent to military-style camps throughout the nation, a welcome labor force to take the place of those who went to war.

The "work of national importance" included improving soil conservation, planting trees, helping in mental institutions, fighting forest fires and doing the vital farm and dairy work that fed the nation and the soldiers. Some COs voluntarily served as human guinea pigs for medical experiments.

Almost all of the sixty-seven camps nationwide were set up with the aid of the National Service Board for Religious Objectors, with representation from the three denominations primarily involved—Mennonite, Brethren Church and the American Friends Service Committee. Whereas the majority of the camps were managed by the religious service committees, four were operated directly by the government for those who did not wish to be in a religious environment.

Because workers at Civilian Conservation Corps (CCC) camps had gone to war, the government converted CCC camps for use by the Civilian Public Service (CPS). One of those camps, number 33, was near Fort Collins.

Charles Frantz, a worker at the local camp, which he called Buckingham, wrote faithfully to his family in Rocky Ford, Colorado. A Mennonite, he had found himself in what he described as "a desolate place," redeemed only partially by the nightly basketball games. A day's hard work was very tiring, he said. The men prepared irrigation ditches by laying concrete on the bottom, along with other soil and water conservation tasks.

Forty men lived in each barrack; five barracks ringed the camp. Although they were fed and given suitable clothing, the men were not paid for their labor. They were allotted time for spiritual guidance and reflection and for personal development.

Each individual was consigned to a three-year enrollment, which meant that the camps did not close when the war ended. Frantz wrote longingly of the end of his time at the camp, which came about a year after the war in the Pacific ended. One group of COs helped deliver supplies to Europe in the aftermath of the war.

While traveling, a local resident encountered a woman who reported that her Amish father had been in camp 33 but was unable to find a trace of the camp when he returned years later. Only historic records and memory survive.

Another Lost Mountain Camp

Although no one can pinpoint the exact location of Camp Horn in upper Poudre Canyon, several longtime residents and historians agree that it did exist for a time in the late 1920s and/or early '30s. Sponsored by the City of Greeley, it was a basic Boy Scout camp, mainly tents, for a few years—like CPS #33, precise dates cannot be identified, and no trace of the camp remains.

Dreher Pickle Factory

William Dreher knew pickles. Dills, sweet pickles, gherkins and other varieties were processed at the Denver plant he founded in 1904. But the city grew and the cucumber fields moved farther away, so in 1921, he sold his Denver operation and moved to Fort Collins, buying a five-acre farm on North Taft Hill Road.

Not just any cucumber is suitable for pickling. The vegetable must be just the right size (not too big or too small) and at the right stage of maturity and, ideally, have a bumpy skin. Small cucumbers become gherkins; larger ones can be processed sliced or whole. The pickling process is also precise and delicate. Dreher knew just what to do.

He started by selling pickles in small quantities, but success soon led him to purchase six acres on the north side of Riverside Drive at Mulberry Street, where he built a salting station in the early 1920s. The location was good, with the railroad close by. Salting vats made from redwood railroad ties lined the street side of the facility, and their contents perfumed the air. Local farmers began growing cucumbers to supply the vats, and for a time, both enterprises were thriving, with farmers regularly selling their crops and local

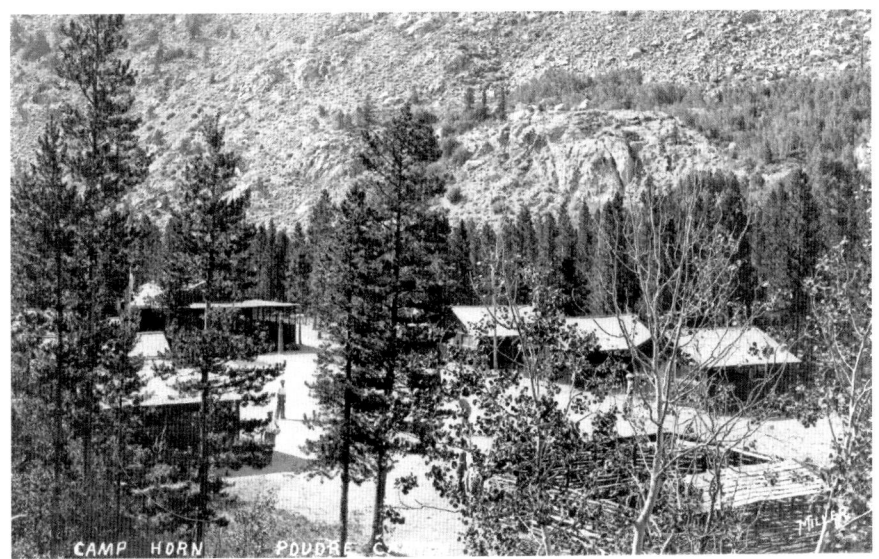

Camp Horn. *MEM*.

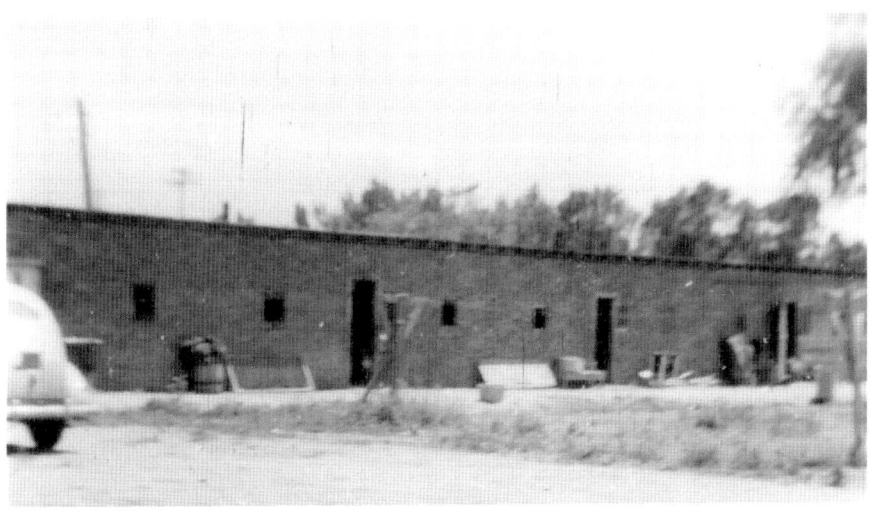

Dreher Pickle Factory. *LHA 97120_00_007B*.

workers finding employment—although migrant workers were imported to harvest the cucumbers, as there were many more fields than local workers could handle.

The company also pickled peppers and processed horseradish.

Dreher died in 1933, leaving his sons, Fred, William, Robert and Thomas, in charge of the plant. In 1946, the company announced plans for a processing plant next to the vats. At some point, the Dreher Company donated land to the city for the sewage processing facility. By 1975, the sons had sold the factory to the Western Foods Processing Company, which continued making pickles here until 1989, when the cucumber supply became unreliable; the plant was relocated to La Junta. For a couple of years after Western Foods bought the plant, local residents could go to the factory and get oversized cucumbers for free.

Shortly after the plant had relocated, a fire gutted much of the facility here. The city bought the land and what remained of the factory in 1995; it was discovered that so many years of pickle salting had rendered the land unsuitable for commercial use. In 2008, the remains of the facility were torn down.

Today, people who have lived here long enough might sometimes spare a nostalgic glance at the spot that once held the pickle factory as they drive by, recalling with fondness a pungent part of Fort Collins's past.

Statues and Symbols

At the corner of Linden and Walnut Streets, the Benevolent and Protective Order of Elks (BPOE) built a two-story structure in 1903 to house its organization. In the front lobby, informing all comers of the identity of its present occupants, stood a stately mounted elk. The BPOE later moved to a building on Remington Street that had formerly been a YMCA and was rebuilt following a devastating downtown explosion in the 1970s. In the new century, it relocated once again to a building on East Mulberry Street.

A sculpture of a dinosaur stood along Interstate 25 for many years, advertising the unique, locally renowned Swetsville Zoo in Timnath. The "animals" in the zoo were all created by Bill Swets, who welded metals and pieces of machinery together to create the sculptures that included a "heavy metal" band and a space cowboy. Sadly, the roadside creature was destroyed by an errant motorist in 2009.

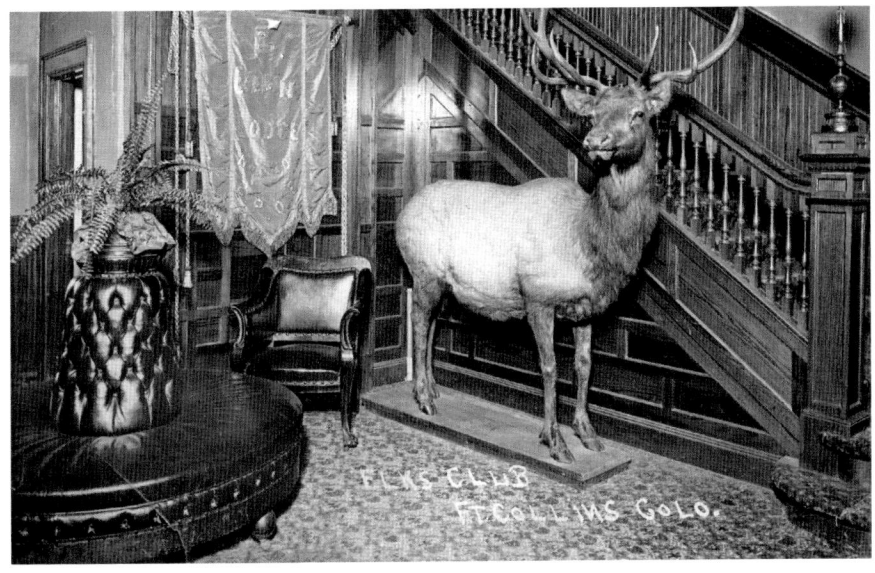

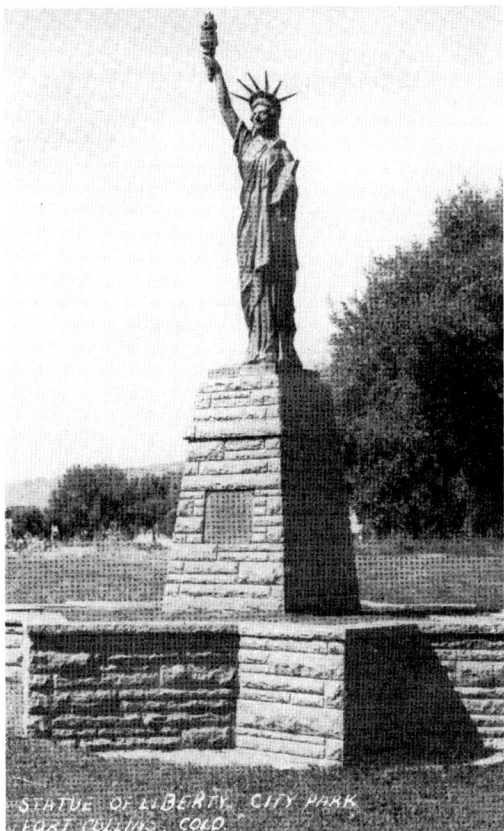

Above: Elks Club lobby. *MEM.*

Left: City Park Statue of Liberty. *MEM.*

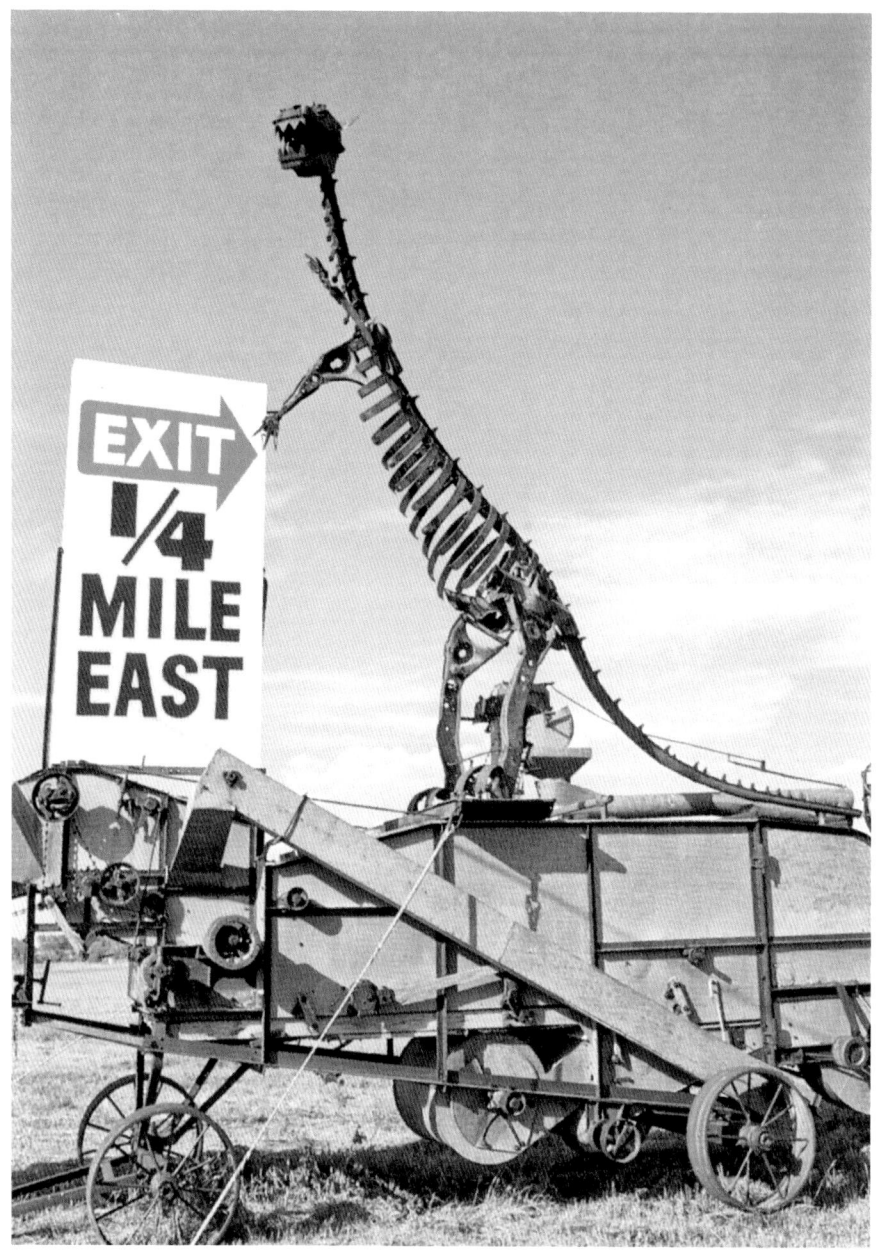

The Swetsville dinosaur on I-25. *Courtesy of Angeline Swets and Bill Swets.*

In 1955, a local Boy Scout troop built a platform to hold a replica Statue of Liberty in City Park, along the shores of Sheldon Lake. Originally made of copper, the statue—one of many made available by the U.S. government to Boy Scout troops around the country—was replaced in 1985 after years of wear and tear. Using the first statue as a mold, Richard and Heidi Eversley of Northern Colorado Art Facility created a new bronze statue on a sandstone pedestal. Several individuals and local organizations made the replacement statue, dedicated July 4, 1985, a reality. The plaque honors contributors.

Home of the Romeros

Adobe, once a common construction material in the arid Southwest and still in use in many parts of the world, usually consists of clay soil, sand, straw and water. Packed densely into forms, the mixture hardens into solid, heavy bricks that warm the house in winter and cool it in summer.

At the time John Romero set out to build his house in 1927, adobe was the most affordable material. Before they moved into the house, John and Inez Rivera Romero lived in a converted boxcar, a benefit of his job with Union Pacific. But the couple wanted a real home.

Advised by a friend from New Mexico, Romero constructed his small house at 425 Tenth Street in Andersonville. By 1935, the house had four rooms, including a dirt-floor cold room for storing produce and eggs and a cozy kitchen where Inez prepared delicious meals to feed their seven children. The house often smelled like fresh-baked bread, one relative recalls. With her treadle machine, Inez sewed clothes for her family from flour sacks.

Though electricity came sometime in the 1930s to Andersonville, Buckingham and Alta Vista, the three northeast neighborhoods populated mainly by Hispanics and clustered near the Great Western Sugar Factory, indoor plumbing was slower to arrive. Despite these drawbacks, one daughter, Francis, born in that decade, recalls a warm, loving, happy home with a mother devoted to her family and a father who worked hard to provide for them. Like many another Hispanic men, Romero worked in the sugar beet factory for a number of years, sometimes taking night shifts so he could hold down another job as well.

It was a close neighborhood in those years, Francis recalls. People knew and helped one another. In her neighborhood, her father was known as "the mayor," the one people came to with problems, and he was also a notary.

An involved citizen, he encouraged his friends and neighbors to vote. Most families had gardens and kept chickens on their small plots. When Mrs. Romero wanted a little peace and quiet, she would tell the children to pray and then go outside to play.

After Inez's death, the house sat vacant until preservationists, concerned about the loss of the only remaining adobe house in Andersonville, organized to save it. Under the auspices of the Poudre Landmarks Foundation and thanks to the City of Fort Collins, community groups, businesses and dedicated volunteers, in 2006, after considerable restorative work, the home of the Romeros became the Museo de las Tres Colonias, a place where memorabilia and representations of a rich cultural heritage are honored and preserved. Now brightly painted, the museum is open to the public one Saturday a month. Walking around in the small space, one can almost hear the echoes of children's voices, high and light, smell the baking bread and feel the love.

Chapter 7
SOME TWENTIETH-CENTURY TALES

This collection of columns and vignettes ends with a few more-contemporary tales. The pieces that follow recall significant events that reflect the times in which they occurred and affected the citizens of Fort Collins in various ways. Before the digital revolution, people got news from the newspaper and radio, fleeting reports that quickly passed out of the public consciousness. This chapter brings to life some of those events and people, preserving their memory and capturing their moments in time.

WHEN CARS ARRIVED HERE

"Get a horse!" was the common cry when that new-fangled invention, the automobile, first chugged into town. Certainly, the amazing creation had its proponents along with its detractors, but most people were still using horses to haul conveyances, and the noisy, belching mechanical creatures badly frightened the four-legged beasts.

In his book *The Automobile Comes to Fort Collins*, Malcolm McNeill describes the arrival of the first car, a curved-dash Oldsmobile driven by Judge J. Mack Mills. The judge took the train to Denver to purchase his car for $700 and then drove it back to his home in Fort Collins, arriving, his daughter said, looking like a mud statue.

The automobile circa 1902 was topless, with the steering device on the right—no windshield, no bumpers, no fenders, a hand-cranked starter, brass sidelights for night driving. The engine, located under the single seat, was smaller than that of a contemporary riding mower.

These vehicles had to use rutted wagon roads. No road went directly from Denver to Fort Collins; rather, the roads took a circuitous route through Greeley and Berthoud—in essence, the stagecoach line. No directional or regulatory signs aided drivers. No such thing as a traffic light. No rules of the road.

Mills drove the car around a little with the dealer on board; that was his driving lesson and about as much as any driver got in those days. No license was required, no age limits imposed. Once, on a trip to Estes Park, Mills's daughter, Freda, drove the car whenever her father needed to get out, carrying two rocks to put under the rear wheels if the car began rolling backward. Like Freda, many other women quickly mastered the art of maneuvering an automobile.

These early cars didn't go very fast—the Olds went about ten miles an hour on the better roads. After he had bought the car, Mills spent the night in Berthoud before heading home. It had rained that day, and he had no protection, thus his dramatic mud-covered arrival. Later, when Mills took a trip to Berthoud, a local newspaper congratulated him for making such good time—an hour and five minutes to go twenty miles.

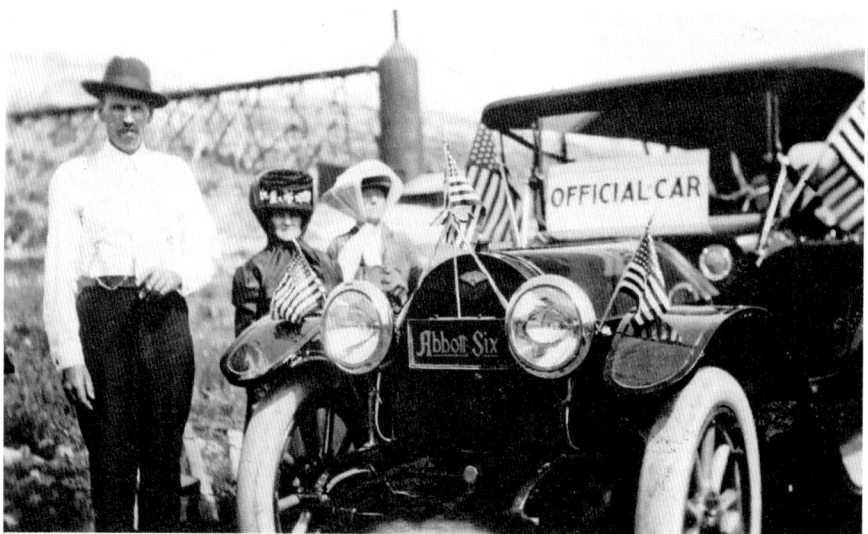

Abbott Six automobile. *MEM.*

Along with horses, dogs were another hazard of the road. At the time, dogs ran loose here; they apparently considered the new machines prey, for they chased cars, sometimes surrounding the offending beasts, and on more than one occasion caused the driver to lose control.

One early model, the Abbott Six shown in this photograph, did not long endure despite its six-cylinder engine and dashing design. Before automobiles were enclosed, women wore protective headgear to ride in them—and to drive them. Not an easy task, for the car had to be started by dint of hard pulls on the starter crank and steered using considerable strength. Still, the unwieldy contraptions caught on with the public. By the next decade, cars were commonplace in town. In 1908, an H.C. Bradley photograph depicted over thirty of the forty-plus vehicles owned here at that time. Like it or not, the automobile had arrived to stay.

Quarantine

In 1911, little was known about the transmission of disease, so when the Greenamyre children came down with scarlet fever, their family doctor could not determine how they might have contracted it. What he could do, however, was place a quarantine sign on the front door, confining mother and children to their home. Howard Greenamyre was advised to leave the home immediately so he could continue to work and support his family.

A bacterial infection, scarlet fever causes a rash, along with a sore throat and fever. Now it is treatable with antibiotics, but there were no antibiotics available when the Greenamyre children became ill. The disease was often serious, sometimes fatal, especially among the very young or the elderly. Not knowing precisely how it was spread, physicians took precautions to ensure that no one else got sick. Thus, the quarantine.

The quarantine, Katherine Greenamyre (one of the children) recalled, lasted six weeks, and the children could not return to school for two more weeks afterward. City physician Dr. Clarkson Taylor said the family could not return library books, send out mail or hang clothes out to dry. Could clothes be sent to the laundry? Only if they were first boiled for twenty minutes (rather hard on fabric) was the reply.

The school was fumigated. All the students in grades three, six and eight at Laurel School were sent home, and the rooms were filled with smoking formaldehyde—a smell that lingered when the students returned to school the next day. The kindergarten room at Remington School was fumigated as well.

Friends came by to talk to the children through the windows. One friend told Katherine that an assigned essay on temperance that she had worked hard on had been burned lest it transmit the infection.

When the doctor came to check on the patients, he put on an enveloping smock, which he had sterilized in the bathroom sink. Upon departing, he hung it on the back porch to dry.

Flowers and cards arrived for the patients. Though Katherine doesn't mention it in her book *Let Me Take You Back with Me*, food was no doubt delivered from the grocery store. But the family's husband and father was not allowed to see his wife and children.

Katherine's mother had feared the worst, knowing of a child who had died of scarlet fever a few months earlier and of another who became deaf because of the illness. She knew that the disease could cause long-term complications. But the four Greenamyre children survived the siege, two of them with mild cases and two more severely stricken. At last the quarantine was lifted, and normal life began again.

Nature Unleashed

Early in December 1913, it began to snow. And snow. And snow. All over the Front Range. At first, the snowfall did not seem unusual or alarming, but by the end of the first week in December, it had turned into a blizzard. About three feet of snow fell here, but the big problem was the wind, which whipped the snow around, creating great piles of white stuff everywhere, drifts higher than horses or people.

Schools closed. Businesses closed. Farmers struggled to reach their livestock to feed them. Not even the large Woeber trolley cars, with their broad metal cattle catchers in front, could get through the drifts. Railroad tracks, buried in snow, were cleared by horse-drawn plows—only those sturdy beasts were powerful enough to break through the drifts. In one case, sixteen horses pulled a single plow. No sooner would the track be cleared than drifts would bury it again. Automobile traffic, such as it was, came to a complete standstill. The relatively new vehicles were not built to deal with deep snow. Mail could not be delivered.

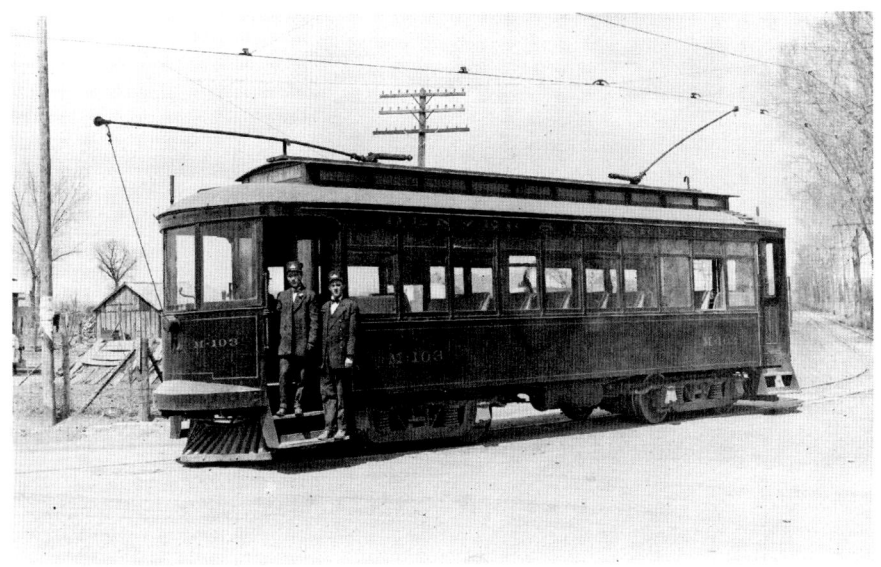

Interurban Woeber trolley. *MEM.*

Unable to withstand the weight of the snow, some roofs caved in. In one instance, a stabled horse was caught under the debris but managed to get out, apparently unharmed. Most homes were heated with coal, delivered by train. The coal supply was getting dangerously low before the trains started running regularly again; families huddled together to keep warm. The fire chief warned of the danger of fires that could not be contained because the sites were inaccessible.

Cut off from the rest of the world, residents of Estes Park were in a desperate situation, with food and supplies nearly gone and power lines down. It was a week before help managed to get through from Lyons. Deer and other wildlife were seen mingling with domestic livestock looking for forage.

Here in Fort Collins, the curfew bell sounded as usual at 8:00 p.m. on Thursday and Friday nights, warning children to be off the streets. A local newspaper noted that in spite of the storm and the fact that no adult was out, let alone children, the bell ringer nonetheless managed to get to his post and do his duty.

For a time, the only system still working was the telephone. At the central office, operators heroically stayed on the job several days, trying to keep communication lines open. So intense and exhausting was the effort that two operators fainted at their desks.

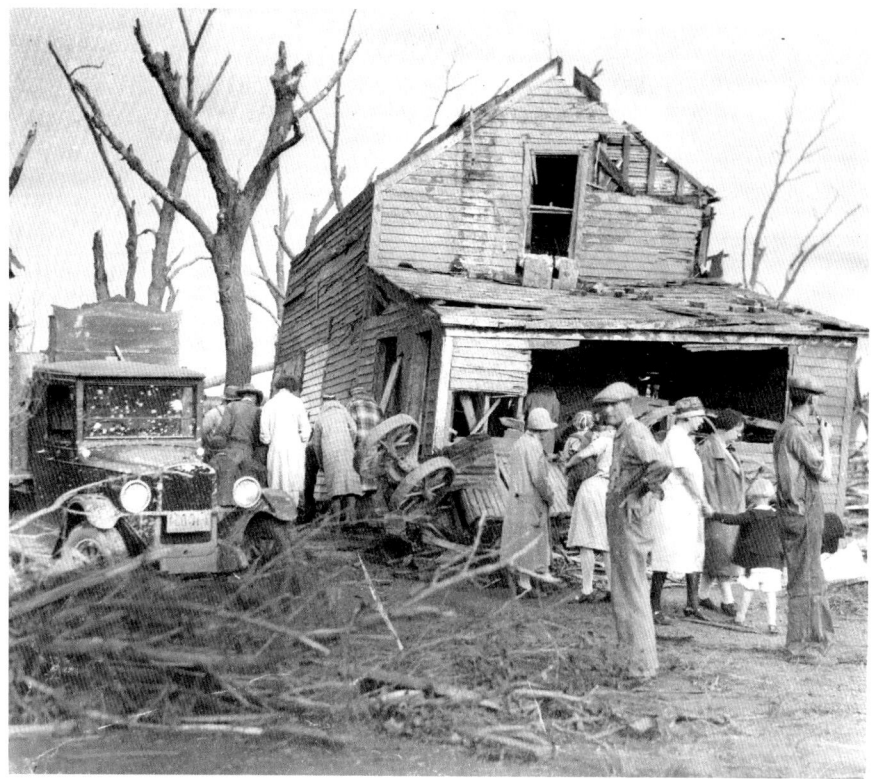

Damage from the Johnstown tornado. *MEM*.

It was a full month before life returned to normal, systems functioned again and the toll of damage could be reckoned. Denver, hit much harder than northern Colorado, fared the worst, but Fort Collins did not get off lightly. Even though there have been memorable crippling snowstorms since then, this one is still remembered after more than one hundred years.

A different kind of natural disaster, but equally devastating, happened in a small town near Fort Collins in July 1928. Although tornadoes are rare along the Front Range in Colorado, they do occur and can be devastating. A massive twister passed through Johnstown, a small township south and east of Fort Collins, causing loss of life and considerable destruction. This photograph shows a sampling of the damage the storm did to that small northern Colorado community. Lacking the warning systems in place today, the residents were completely unprepared. Tornados have happened as nearby as Wellington, north of town, and on land east of Fort Collins, though none has been as deadly as this one.

Airplane Crash

While the Second World War raged on far away, Americans did not know the constant fear of hearing airplanes overhead and bracing for the destruction they would bring. Here in this area, far from either coast, no one was accustomed to seeing planes crash or bombs falling. Pilots and crew, it was assumed, flew and died in the heat of battle, not at home.

However, sometimes airmen did die on the homefront. Those on the homefront might have tended to forget that pilots needed to train somewhere and occasionally something went wrong.

On October 18, 1943, such a tragedy happened very close to home. A local ranch wife, Mrs. Albert Chandler, was going about her daily routine that morning when she heard "a violent explosion" that shattered her peace. She promptly reported the incident to the county sheriff, Ray Barger, who announced in the newspaper the next day that a B-17 bomber from Lowry Field in Aurora was missing. Drivers were asked to stay away from roads to the crash site, which was at the northeastern tip of Rocky Mountain National Park.

To get to the site of the crash, rescue crews had to make their way through difficult terrain, not a place where vehicles would be useful. They had to navigate heavily forested areas that were blanketed in snow on horseback, ascending peaks as high as eleven thousand feet.

The B-17, which initially was labeled the B-299, was made by Boeing Aircraft to carry bombs long distances, defending such outposts as Alaska and Hawaii from distant bases. Its 103-foot wingspan made it the largest military aircraft of the time; journalists had named it the "Flying Fortress." By 1943, it was widely used to bomb targets in Germany, with the majority of the planes returning safely from their missions.

But something unknown had gone wrong with this airplane, which had a crew of eight on board. In their book *Walking into Colorado's Past*, authors Ben Fogelberg and Steve Grinstead note that newspapers never offered an explanation for the crash.

The searchers got within a mile of the wreckage, south and east of the Pingree Park campus off Poudre Canyon road, and walked the rest of the way in. Leaking fuel had started a fire, which forest rangers were able to put out quickly. They found five airmen's bodies and carried them back to the horses—"tedious and grim" work, reported the *Fort Collins Express-Courier.*

Within two days, the searchers had found the remaining three bodies and brought them out, leaving behind debris from the wreckage.

"Whatever happened," the authors say, "one thing is certain. Its crew died at the same time US soldiers were fighting and dying...elsewhere. The wreckage...must be regarded as one more place where young men died in service to their country."

Another Who Served

When Fort Collins native Stanley Sepulveda returned home from service in the Second World War, for which he received a Good Conduct Medal, an Honorable Service Button, a Driver and Mechanic Badge and a Victory Medal, he entered a restaurant downtown and was refused service. Discrimination against Hispanics had long been common in downtown establishments; after the war, a number of individuals lobbied to have discriminatory signs removed. While working in the maintenance department at the college, Sepulveda became an advocate for rights for Hispanics and served on the Human Rights Commission.

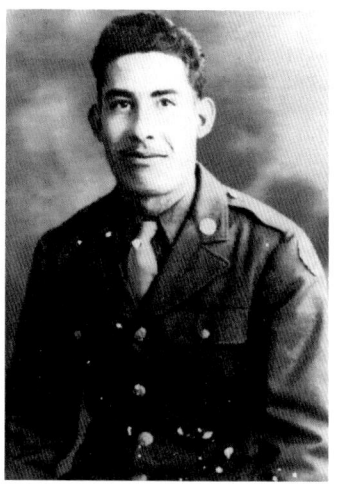

Stanley Sepulveda. *Courtesy of Stanley Sepulveda.*

Spanish-American Baseball League

They worked in the baking sun all day, weeding, thinning plants and, later, topping the sugar beets that provided their livelihood. Little in the way of entertainment was available for the Hispanic beet-field workers who labored through the long, hot summer days, only the youngest children not in the fields. A desire for diversion led to the formation of a baseball league; the local team was the Fort Collins Legionnaires.

In the depths of the Great Depression, young men among these laborers created the Rocky Mountain Spanish-American Baseball League. In northern Colorado, teams often played on cow pastures, uneven ground filled with ruts, cow pies and holes. Their equipment was mostly handmade;

base bags were gunnysacks filled with dirt, baseballs were twine wound tightly and gloves were made from rags. But the players were happy to have the chance to test their skills, and families were happy to watch them play. At that time in America, baseball was the number-one sport in the country, followed and loved by millions.

Players liked coming to Fort Collins because the field at City Park was smooth and free of hazards, with real base bags, bats and balls. Games were held in several towns in the area—Greeley, Ault and Brighton, to name a few—but none had such a good field as the one here.

At the time these leagues formed in several states, Major League Baseball (MLB) was still firmly segregated. Once Jackie Robinson and the Brooklyn Dodgers broke the color barrier in 1947, Hispanic baseball leagues gradually became outdated, and it was not long before a few of the best players in these leagues were being recruited to MLB. Just as the Negro leagues were a proving ground for Robinson and others, players in the Hispanic leagues emerged from their time on the ball fields with the skills to make it in the Majors despite the many obstacles in their paths.

Over time, as opportunities in professional baseball increased, the leagues disbanded. Though play continued for a time, the northern Colorado league formally ended in 1970. Yet in these summer days when hometown ball fields are once again filled with players of all ages, echoes from those long-ago days of the Spanish-American Baseball League reverberate resoundingly down through the decades.

Coal Strike

In the dead of winter in 1949, John L. Lewis, he of the shaggy eyebrows and bulldog chin, brought our coal-burning nation to its knees.

President of the United Mine Workers of America, he had called strikes before, but this one was especially difficult. Most people still heated with coal, and industry largely functioned on it. Steam locomotives still rode the rails. No one escaped the effects of this strike, which began just after Christmas and dragged on, in various stages of resistance, until early March 1950.

In Fort Collins as elsewhere, people rationed their dwindling supplies of coal and purchased as much as they could when coal was available. Some farsighted homeowners had already converted to natural gas, no doubt pleased to bring an end to the messy job of shoveling coal into their furnaces, but most had not. Nor had schools, built many decades before. After a run on small electric space heaters carried by hardware stores, no more could be had. Without coal, officials had no choice but to shut down the public schools. The college closed as well. Never known for their warmth even before the strike, the old buildings on campus were uninhabitable when unheated. Maintenance crews did all they could to prevent freezing pipes. Shops and restaurants closed. Along with the rest of the country, Fort Collins hunkered down to survive as best the people could.

When Harry S Truman became president in 1945, he inherited a simmering cauldron of labor disputes that boiled over after the end of World War II. By 1949, he was losing patience with the strikers, threatening a federal takeover of essential services and invoking the full power of the law to force miners back to work. All of which seemed irrelevant to people trying to keep warm. The winter was an especially harsh one, with frequent snow and freezing temperatures. Whether or not people were sympathetic with the mine workers' cause—better pay, shorter hours and safer conditions, among other issues—and many were, they grew less so as the strikes continued. The unrelieved cold was particularly hard on the elderly, the ill and the very young. Some parts of the country quickly became denuded of available wood.

Even when Lewis called a halt to the strikes, wildcat strikes continued at several mines. Labor had risen up to make its voice heard.

But it was Lewis's last hurrah; he never again led such a protracted, massive strike, and his influence faded. Accelerating a transformation already underway, homeowners increasingly converted to natural gas, railroad companies opted for diesel fuel and business and industry moved away from coal furnaces. While coal maintained a significant role in the country's infrastructure, the strikes had brought about a sea change as time-honored practices gave way to progress.

The end of the strikes, along with the arrival of spring, brought on a long, thankful, collective sigh of relief.

Galloping Goose

Oh, how Fort Collins folks loved their little galloping goose, the trolley that took them all around town. The nickname came about because of the streetcar's slight up-and-down motion as it trotted along the tracks. Children wore tokens, which had holes for just such a purpose, around their necks so as not to lose them. A ride cost five cents.

Along with the turn-of-the-century arrival of the automobile came more sophisticated forms of public transportation, including streetcars. The populace was eagerly embracing new technologies at the dawn of a new century. Streetcars first came to Fort Collins, one of the smallest cities in America to have this convenience, in 1907. The first cars here were heavy Denver and Interurban (D&I) cars—large lumbering vehicles with a cowcatcher in front. Traffic was not controlled in the early 1900s; drivers generally stayed right but sometimes veered into the middle of the street, and streetcars and automobiles sometimes had encounters, not to mention the horse-drawn wagons that still appeared in town. Pity the poor pedestrian.

In 1919, the Woeber Company went bankrupt. Left without public transportation, the citizens of Fort Collins voted to buy the system in order to restore service. It was decided to purchase newer, smaller Birney cars, which had steering at each end and moved about efficiently. Residents fell in love with the little cars, of which the Fort Collins Municipal Railway System once owned seven, with five in service at the same time. Passersby loved to watch three cars change places at the downtown intersection of Mountain and College Avenues.

Anyone who lived here during the time of the trolley has a story to tell. Abiding stories include the way conductors would stop in the middle of the street to pick up or let out passengers, conductors who allowed a passenger to ride even if he or she didn't have a nickel and the familiar sight of the colorful streetcars, bobbing up and down, full of waving passengers, passing by. Regular passengers knew the schedule by heart; the trolleys were nearly always on time. Fort Collins became the last town in America to still have operating Birneys, the fare still five cents.

Sadly, the love affair did not last. In 1951, prosperous and enamored of automobiles, the citizens of Fort Collins voted to end streetcar service in favor of motorized transportation. Today, the restored Car 21 still "gallops" from downtown to City Park in the summer, a lingering vestige of a time long past.

Homegrown Entertainment

After she retired from her many years as a speech and drama professor at the college, Ruth Jocelyn Wattles, known to one and all as RJ, started a local theater company. With the goal of bringing the college community and the townspeople amicably together, the Town and Gown Theater blended the two entities by having the rehearsals and performances at Old Main Theater and inviting townspeople to audition for parts, help with stagecraft and attend the shows.

In 1954, the group presented *The Women* by Clare Booth Luce. Among other productions, the company presented *Seven Keys to Baldpate*, *If Men Played Cards as Women Do* and *The Madwoman of Chaillot*. The group stayed together for several years; in the 1970s, another community theater, OpenStage, still a going concern, met a wider need.

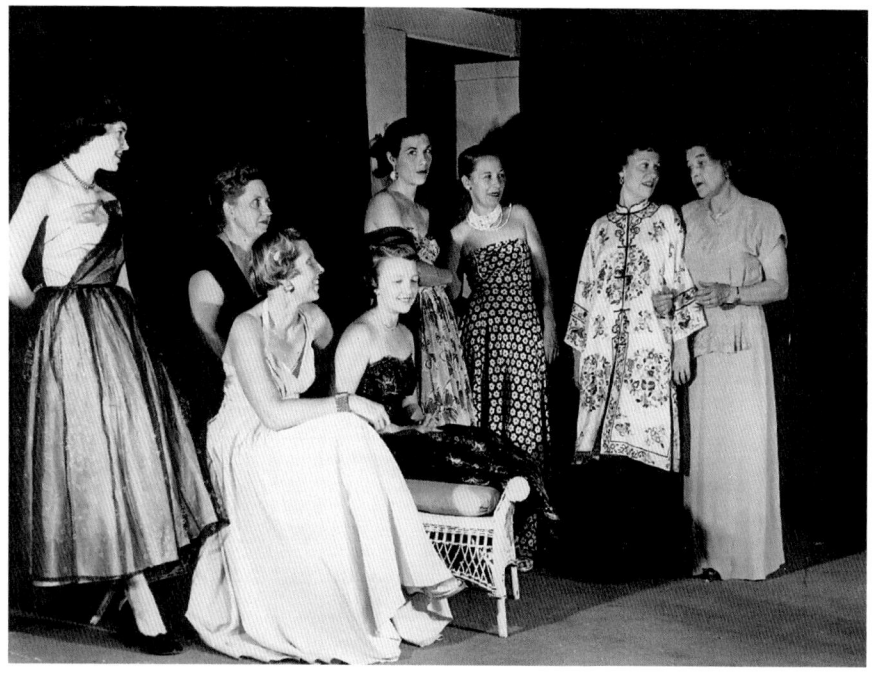

Cast of *The Women*, *from left*: Carolyn Stimmel, Dorothy McComb, Emily Wilmarth, unidentified, Yvonne Jones, Mona Atteberry, unidentified and Margaret Stimmel. *Author's collection.*

Mrs. Roosevelt Makes a Visit

August 8, 1958, was a memorable day in Fort Collins—Eleanor Roosevelt came to town. With her grandson Elliott Roosevelt Jr. graduating from Colorado State University, she had agreed to be the commencement speaker.

Landing at Christman Field from a private plane piloted by her son Elliott, who lived in Meeker at the time, she was greeted with flowers and a welcome from the mayor and his wife, Mr. and Mrs. Robert Sears; CSU president William Morgan and his wife, Lilla; and Walter Cooper, representing the State Board of Agriculture, who escorted her to Green Hall for a press conference.

During the 1950s, the United States was entangled in the Cold War with the USSR. Led by Nikita Khrushchev, that nation sought to spread communism throughout the world; indeed, Khrushchev had informed the former first lady that communism was the inevitable future. This challenge created among our nation's leaders, and in Roosevelt, a somber mood, for Khrushchev's threat was taken seriously.

At a press conference, she spoke to the need for a "solid" Middle East policy, which included strong support for Israel and use of the United Nations "as it was intended to be used," a center for mediation and international cooperation. She noted that part of the difficulty in dealing with the Middle East was a lack of understanding of Arabian culture, beliefs and lifestyles. Communism need not take over the world, Roosevelt told the 106 graduates: their charge was to work for the furtherance and preservation of democracy in this country and elsewhere. She challenged them to take responsibility for ensuring a democratic future.

As part of the graduation ceremony, she received an honorary doctor of laws degree. Known throughout the world for her humanitarian work, Roosevelt had served as the first American delegate to the United Nations and was the author of several books, along with a daily syndicated newspaper column, "My Day." But her greater pleasure that day was seeing her grandson receive a bachelor of science degree in animal husbandry.

Few present that day (besides his widow and son) may have known that Roosevelt's husband, Franklin, was in Fort Collins for a brief time in 1920 while campaigning for vice president on the Democratic ticket as James M. Cox's running mate. Most present that day probably knew that the Cox-Roosevelt ticket lost to Warren G. Harding. When FDR came to Fort Collins, he spoke from the balcony of the Northern Hotel,

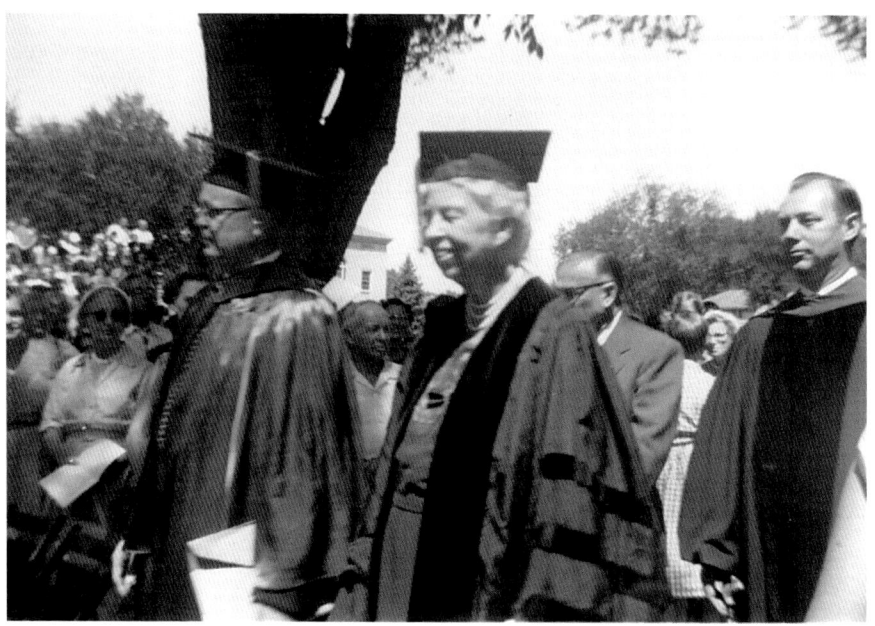

Eleanor Roosevelt (college president William Morgan at left) at Colorado State University. *Courtesy of Ed Lucero.*

near the railroad station. Not yet paralyzed by polio, he had embarked on a vigorous campaign tour that included local "whistle stops." If his wife accompanied him, history does not record her presence, so it is almost certainly safe to claim the 1958 visit here as her first—and only—appearance in Fort Collins.

Father Goose

Geese on the grass; geese waddling across the street, holding up traffic; geese flying in a ragged V shape, honking as they go; geese leaving their calling cards—these birds are an integral part of our town. Whether residents love them or not, they are here to stay.

In the 1930s, the federal government declared that hunters could no longer use live decoys. A captive flock of Canada geese residing in the suburb Bow Mar, near Denver, for that very purpose suddenly became problematic. What to do with them? Some suggested killing them, but the human residents did not like that idea. Consequently, they were bought and relocated to nearby Bowles Lake. But without the migrating gene, the flock continued to propagate and within a couple of decades had once again become a problem.

Enter Gurney Crawford, a wildlife biologist who worked for what is now the state Division of Wildlife and lived in Fort Collins. Crawford loved all birds (except crows). Fort Collins had very few geese; it seemed logical to start a resident flock here. He and his colleagues William Rutherford and Jack Grieb collected eggs from the nests, transporting them to Crawford's home in insulated boxes kept warm with hot-water bottles and giving them to banty hens to hatch. Result: surprised banty hens and the beginnings of a Fort Collins flock.

Once incubators were procured, the biologists experimented to find the right food for the goslings, an even balance of protein and carbs, to allow their wings to lift them aloft. Too much protein made the feathers too heavy; too little left the feathers too light. With the help of Ranchway Feeds, they soon developed a nutritious mixture. The flock began to prosper.

Then came more problems to solve: geese will build a nest just about anywhere on the ground, leaving the eggs prey to raccoons, foxes and skunks. Although geese are fierce in their defense of a nest, eggs were still getting taken. So Crawford built nesting platforms inaccessible to predators. The platforms worked; soon, our own resident flock was well established. The birds having no patterning to migrate, they were perfectly content right here.

Before long, Canada geese on their way south began to stop by. There was plenty to eat here, and it looked like a likely spot to spend the winter, so many of them did just that instead of migrating farther south. Hunters in southern New Mexico who had been expecting the migrants were chagrined when they failed to appear. Though the biologists had not intended to increase the flock in such a way, the geese had made their choice.

Although development and consequent loss of habitat have affected the resident flocks as well as the winter "tourists," a stable population of geese continues to flourish here.

Crawford was honored for his conservation efforts. Decades after his death, his legacy continues, munching, waddling, flying, honking and nesting in their year-round happy home.

Cloverleaf Kennel Club

Locals called it the cloverleaf—the symmetrical, circular design engineered to make the intersection of U.S. Highways 34 and 287 at Loveland safer. So naturally, when a greyhound racing group decided to build a dog track at that spot in 1955, it could only be called the Cloverleaf Kennel Club.

At the time, gambling was legal in Colorado only at this dog track and at Mile High in Commerce City, making it an attractive venue for thousands of hopeful spectators who placed their bets there. On occasion, Cloverleaf was reported to have drawn as many as ten thousand spectators. The track was lit up so brightly that its lights could be seen for miles in every direction. The vast parking lot was usually full; it cost five dollars to get in, but parking was free. At the height of racing's popularity, the kennel club added a new grandstand and offered refreshment stands, restrooms and box seats for special patrons.

Not too long after the track was built, the cloverleaf went away as I-25 emerged in the 1960s, one mile at a time.

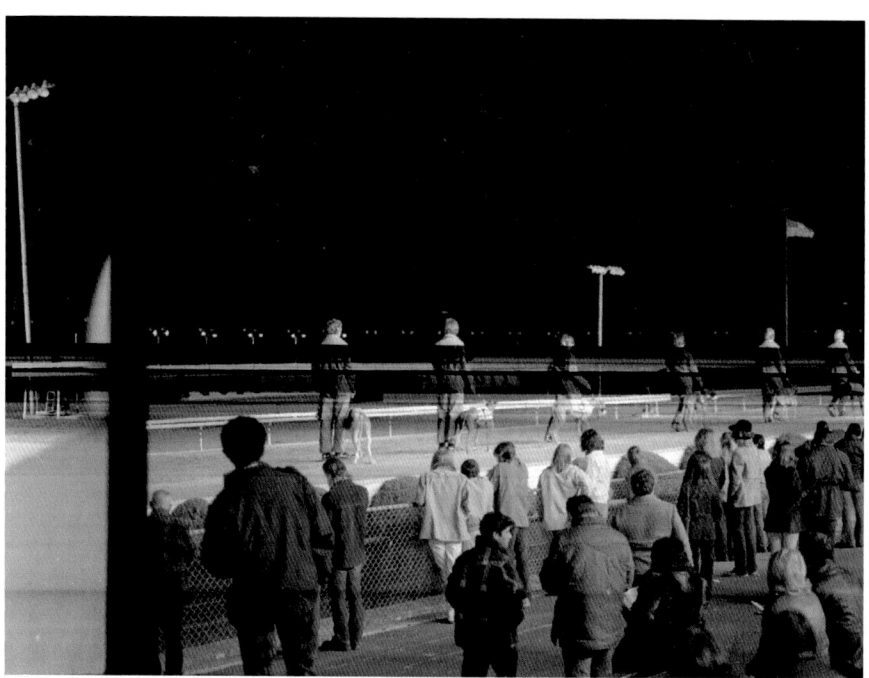

Cloverleaf Kennel Club. *LHA T02942c.*

One former fan recalled that trumpets announced each race. Released to chase the prey, eight dogs lined up at the starting post eager to catch Whizmo, the electric rabbit that was always just a tantalizing distance ahead of them, even though the dogs could run as fast as forty miles an hour. Sometimes there would be a photo finish, leaving judges to determine win, place and show. After every race, a scoreboard displayed the payouts. Winners hurried to the windows to collect their take, while losers tore up their tickets, tossed them on the floor and debated whether to try again.

Times change, technology steadily advances and public interests wax and wane. Along with animal-rights groups' concerns came, in 1991, legal gambling in Central City, Black Hawk and Cripple Creek, putting an end to the exclusivity the tracks had enjoyed. The venue was soon competing, too, with off-track betting and online betting via the Internet—no need to go out and stand in the heat or the rain to watch the dogs run. Gradually, revenue declined and crowds dwindled. The heyday of greyhound racing in Colorado had come and gone.

The last race at Cloverleaf was run in June 2006, according to the *Loveland Reporter-Herald*, and two years later, the equipment and furnishings (including Whizmo) went up for auction. By 2012, all traces of the former track had been removed, whereupon Poudre Valley Health Systems began building a new hospital on the grounds, which had earlier been purchased from the McWhinney development company.

Today, few would know that once upon a time a dog track stood on the land now occupied by office buildings and a hospital. Memories, some recorded, some not, are all that remain.

BIBLIOGRAPHY

Ahlbrandt, Arlene, and Mary Hagen. *Women to Remember of Northern Colorado.* Fort Collins, CO: Azure Publishing, Inc., 2001.

Fogelberg, Ben, and Steve Grimstad. *Walking into Colorado's Past.* Englewood, CO: Westcliffe Publishing, 2006.

Fry, Norman. *Cache la Poudre: The River.* Fort Collins, CO: self-published, 1954.

Greenamyre, Helen. *Let Me Take You Back with Me.* Allenspark, CO: Viv's Originals, 1991.

Hansen, James. *Democracy's College in the Centennial State.* Fort Collins: Colorado State University, 1977.

Myrick, Herbert. *Cache la Poudre: The Romance of a Tenderfoot in the Days of Custer.* Fort Collins, CO, 1905.

Pennock, Iola. *Happy Hardships.* Fort Collins, CO, 1982.

Sarchet, Fancher. *Murder and Mirth.* Fort Collins, CO: Sage Publishing, 1956.

Watrous, Ansel. *History of Larimer County, Colorado.* Fort Collins, CO, 1911.

INDEX

A

Allen, Asaph 102
Allison, Inga 89
Arthur, James 48

B

Baker, Jim 18
Barney, Hiram 24
Batterson, Billy 57
Bennett, Thomas 66
Bird, Isabella 32
Boothroyd, Edith 53
Borrell Gang 21
Buss, George 26

C

Camp Horn 112
Carter-Cotton, Francis 51
Chambers, Robert 20
Coffin, Roy 13
Crawford, Gurney 132–133
Crose, Newton 73–74

D

Dickerson, Alice and Helen 55–57
Dreher, William 112–114

F

Frantz, Charles 111

G

Gardner, William 71–72
Goldwater, Barry 61
Greenamyre, Katherine 121

INDEX

H

Hanna, Eddie 93–94
Happy Jack 23
Haystack Rock 99

I

Ideal Cement 71
Ingleside quarry 69

J

Johnstown 124

K

Kelly, Jimmy 29, 30
Kennedy, John F. 61
Kinikinik 101
Koenig, Hazel Ramsey 41

L

Lamb, Elkanah 38
Lewis, John L. 127
Lobato, Jovita 86

M

Makepeace, Laura 83
Masters, Mrs. E.A. 37
Mathews, John 64
McDonald, Ruth Burnett 61–62

Meredith, James 79
Miller, Harvey 74–76
Miller, Luther 104
Miller, Nora Rice 52–53
Miller, Robert 68
Mills, Mack 119
Mitchell Well fire 71
Morton, "Dad" 58

N

Norman, Grafton 85

P

Parker, Billy 61
Provost, John 18

R

Remington School 91, 93
Richart, William 68, 71
Romero, John 117
Roosevelt, Eleanor 131–132
Ryan, William L. 73–74

S

Salyers, Samuel 77
Sarchet, Fancher 74
Seder Plastics 104
Sepulveda, Stanley 126
Siegel, Julian 106
Smith, Clifford and Viola 77
Stover, Frank 35

INDEX

Strang, Robert 110
Swets, Bill 114

T

Thayer, Kenneth 45
Toliver's 106
Town, William 71–72

V

Vaille, Agnes 107–108

W

Wattles, Ruth 130
Welch Block 34
Whitcomb, Kate 50, 51
White, Byron 61

Z

Ziegler, Watson and Martha 45

About the Author

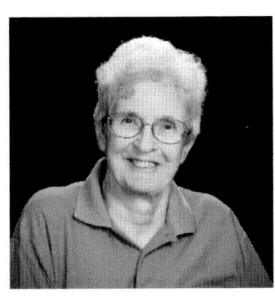

Barbara Fleming, a native of Fort Collins, Colorado, writes a weekly column on local history for the *Fort Collins Coloradoan* newspaper. She has always loved history, an interest she's been able to indulge after retirement from teaching. She is the author or coauthor of several local history books for Arcadia Publishing and one previous book for The History Press, along with a historical novel, *Journeying*, and a Donning Company publication, *Fort Collins: A Pictorial History*. She lives in Old Town Fort Collins with her cat, Shadow. Find her at Facebook.com/localauthorFleming.

Visit us at
www.historypress.net

This title is also available as an e-book